Sea
of
Cimeroth

GOLAN?

Ashtaroth-Karnaim

Apher

M A N A S S

B A

Edrei

(Half Tribe)

RAMOTH-GILEAD

Beth-shean

Jabesh-Gilead

Abel-meholah

Mahanaim

RAMOTH IN GILEAD

Peniel

Jabbok

Succoth

G A L

Ataroth

Zaretan

Mt. Gilead

Betonim

Shittim

Ramoth-mizpeh

Ramoth-gilead

Rabbath

Jaazer

Beth-nimrah

A DAY IN THE LIFE OF ISRAEL WAS MADE POSSIBLE THROUGH THE GENEROUS ASSISTANCE OF:

 THE ASSOCIATION FOR
PROMOTING TOURISM IN ISRAEL

 BANK HAPOALIM

 israel

 ISRAEL DISCOUNT BANK

 EL AL
The Airline of Israel

 THE ISRAEL FUEL CORPORATION LTD.

M
MORIAH HOTELS
Eilat • Tiberias • Dead Sea • Jerusalem • Tel Aviv

 PAZ OIL COMPANY LTD.

 Eastman Kodak Company

 CLAL (ISRAEL) LTD.

TEL AVIV
HILTON

 FEDERATION
OF ISRAELI
CHAMBERS OF
COMMERCE
ISRAEL'S BUSINESS ORGANIZATION

Hertz
"GOING THE EXTRA MILE"
KESHER RENT A CAR LTD.

 **ISCAR LTD.**

OUR SPECIAL THANKS ALSO TO AMIRAM SIVAN, LEON
RECANATI, GIDEON LAHAV, ZADIK BINO, THE LIBERMAN
FAMILY, THE SOCIETY FOR THE PROTECTION OF NATURE IN
ISRAEL, DELTA FILM, APPLE COMPUTER AND ITURIT.

ASSOCIATION
OF LIFE INSURANCE
COMPANIES OF ISRAEL LTD.

ISRAEL
INSURANCE
ASSOCIATION

Sha'ar Hagai NINA BARNETT

Israeli Navy officer candidates practice navigation and patrol skills in inflatable powerboats off the coast of Haifa. **JEFFERY ALLAN SALTER**

A Day in the Life of
Israel

DIRECTED AND EDITED BY
DAVID COHEN

PRODUCED AND CO-EDITED BY
LEE LIBERMAN

DIRECTOR OF PHOTOGRAPHY
PETER HOWE

DESIGNED BY
TOM MORGAN

TEXT BY
SUSAN WELS

CollinsPublishersSanFrancisco
A Division of HarperCollinsPublishers

In his studio in rural Pardes Hanna, near Caesarea, English-born artist
Ardyn Halter rises early to paint an elaborately illustrated *ketubah*, a Hebrew
marriage contract specifying the groom's obligations to his bride.
ROBERT HOLMES

First published in 1994 by Collins Publishers San Francisco.

Copyright © 1994 by Collins Publishers San Francisco
A Day in the Life ® is a registered trademark of HarperCollins Publishers. No
use of this trademark for books, calendars, films or television programs can
be made without prior written consent of the publisher.

*Library of Congress Cataloging-in-Publication Data
A day in the life of Israel / directed and edited by David Cohen ; produced
     and co-edited by Lee Liberman ; designed by Tom Morgan ; text by
     Susan Wels.
          p.   cm.
     ISBN: 0-00-255119-5
     1. Israel—Pictorial works. 2. Israel—Social life and customs—
Pictorial works. I. Cohen, David, 1955- . II. Liberman, Lee
DS108.5.D37 1994
956.94—dc20   94-28746
                                                              CIP
Design: Tom Morgan, Blue Design, San Francisco, California
Printed in Italy. First printing August 1994
10 9 8 7 6 5 4 3 2 1

A child steps out into the morning sunlight from his home inside the labyrinthine walls of old Akko. **RICK RICKMAN**

Pet pigeons roost outside a Bedouin tent near Beersheva.
ANTONIN KRATOCHVIL

I WOULD LIKE TO DEDICATE THIS BOOK TO THE MEMORY OF
LEON LIBERMAN, MY FRIEND AND HUSBAND OF 25 YEARS.
LEON WAS A MAN OF VISION AND OF PASSION. ISRAEL WAS
ONE OF HIS GREAT LOVES.
— LEE LIBERMAN, PRODUCER AND CO-EDITOR

Children from the rural town of Pardes Hanna near Caesarea ride the school bus to Moshav Ammicam. ROBERT HOLMES

INTRODUCTION

I srael is an intense, complex, challenging and ultimately fascinating country. Although it is a small nation, even tiny, it is densely packed with immense geographical diversity; a long, rich history; passionate, fractious politics and a religious and cultural diversity that defies belief. Any attempt to capture every aspect of Israel on film in a single day—even with more than 60 of the world's finest photojournalists—is doomed from the start. It would take hundreds of days and far more pages than we have here.

A Day in the Life of Israel, therefore, is not a comprehensive, evenly balanced view of the country—nor does it pretend to be. It is a compilation of impressions of this ancient and audaciously inventive place, captured on film by 60 highly talented photographers on a single day. This is the 13th book in the Day in the Life series, our Bar Mitzvah book if you will. One hallmark of the Day in the Life series is that it is one of the few places left where photojournalists are given the freedom to shoot what they find the way they want. Nearly all books like this are dictated from the top down. Photographers are given specific directions about what to shoot, and the photographs are edited accordingly. We prefer not to work that way. Instead, we give the photographers general guidance, deploy them geographically, try to provide them with access and contacts, and promise them that if they make a great picture, we will use it.

The advantage to this method, and the one-day formula in general, is that the combination of artistic free-

The new Jewish development of Nazerat Illit crowns a hillside above the old Arab town of Nazareth. **JOEL SARTORE**

dom, intense time restraints and head-to-head competition often produces great pictures. The disadvantage is that subjects which are more important, but less photogenic, are sometimes lost. Therefore, we expect that the pictures in this book will spark controversy, especially in Israel. Fair enough. Israel, filled with passionate people, is a passionate subject. We also expect few to argue with the quality of the photographers' work—something that we are passionate about.

At the same time that we chose pictures for their photographic quality, we tried to keep in mind how much this tiny country means to so many people, particularly the Jews. Israel is, after all, the Jewish homeland, and millions of Jews, in Israel and around the world, toiled mightily, fought bravely and gave generously to establish and preserve this, the last best refuge. Thousands, we must remember, made the ultimate sacrifice.

Photography has its limits, and most of the photographs here do not tell you that modern Israel rose from the ashes of the Holocaust or that it was built under harsh and dangerous conditions. Nor do they tell you that this complex, modern society is in fact a miracle of faith. But every so often, you will see it. In the faces of Russian Jews making *aliyah*, in the gesture of a boy placing a rock at the Holocaust memorial at Yad Vashem, in the bowed head of a soldier at prayer in Jerusalem. These are small moments, but in the words of Israeli poet Yehuda Amichai, they are "saturated with prayers and dreams."

— The Editors

Day in the Life of Israel Photographers and Their Assigned Locations

1. Nubar Alexanian — Jerusalem
2. Shlomo Arad — Ramla
3. Jane Evelyn Atwood — Ramla
4. Shahar Azran — Eilat
5. Micha Bar'Am — Lake Kinneret
6. Anthony Barboza — Dimona, Tel Aviv
7. Nina Barnett — Latrun, Beit Shemesh, Sha'ar Hagai
8. Rick Browne — Caesarea, Herzliya, Netanya
9. Paul Chesley — Jerusalem, Tel Aviv
10. Yossi Cohen — Tel Aviv
11. Barbara DeMoulin — Haluza
12. David Doubilet — Eilat
13. Leonard Freed — The Galil
14. Barry Frydlender — Tel Aviv
15. Avi Ganor — Tel Aviv, The Galil
16. Cristina Garcia Rodero — Jerusalem
17. Shai Ginott — Sde' Boker
18. Yehoshua Glotman — Fassuta, Abbirim
19. C. W. Griffin — Tel Aviv
20. Lori Grinker — Metulla
21. Carol Guzy — The Golan Heights, Tiberias
22. Acey Harper — Hatseva
23. Michal Heiman — Tel Aviv
24. Robert Holmes — Pardes Hanna, Zikhron Ya'acov
25. Yuval Hosen — Tel Aviv
26. Ed Kashi — Hebron
27. Nick Kelsh — Jerusalem
28. Douglas Kirkland — Tel Aviv, Rehovot
29. Antonin Kratochvil — Beersheva
30. Miki Kratsman — Jericho
31. Hiroji Kubota — Zippori
32. Daniel Lainé — Jerusalem
33. Frans Lanting — Hai-Bar, Timna
34. Vera Lentz — Haifa
35. Alex Levac — Safed
36. Gerd Ludwig — Karmiel
37. Pascal Maitre — Isfiya
38. James Marshall — Mitzpe Ramon
39. Susan Meiselas — Shtula, Rosh Hanikra
40. Claus Meyer — Ein Gedi, Masada
41. Gilad Ophir — The Golan Heights
42. Sylvia Plachy — Jaffa
43. Larry Price — Vered Hagalil
44. Eldad Rafaeli — Tel Aviv
45. Raghu Rai — Jerusalem
46. Razi — Kiryat Shemona, The Hula Valley
47. Alon Reininger — Jerusalem
48. Rick Rickman — Akko, Nahariya
49. Steve Rubin — Ashdod
50. David Rubinger — Jerusalem, Tel Aviv
51. Russell Sacks — Kiryat Shaul, Jenin
52. Hana Sahar — Tel Aviv
53. Jeffery Allan Salter — Haifa
54. Emmanuel Santos — B'nei Brak
55. Joel Sartore — Nazareth
56. Moshe Shai — Sodom
57. Duby Tal — Aerials
58. Shabtai Tal — Hazor and Tel Nof Air Force Bases
59. Scott Thode — Taiyiba, Tulkarm, Uhm El Fahm
60. Nik Wheeler — Ashkelon, Gaza Border
61. Marina Yurchenko — Moscow to Tel Aviv
62. Memo Zack — The Golan Heights

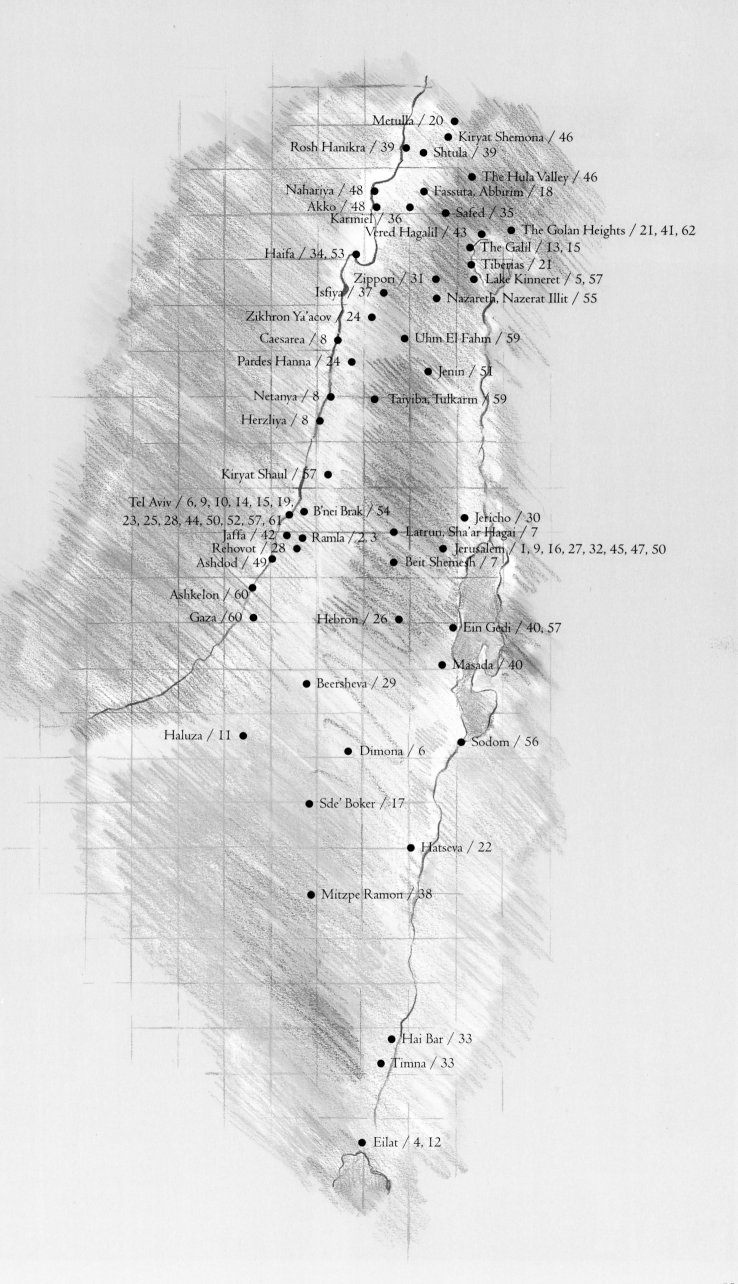

Metulla / 20

Kiryat Shemona / 46

Rosh Hanikra / 39

Shtula / 39

The Hula Valley / 46

Nahariya / 48

Fassuta, Abbirim / 18

Akko / 48

Karmiel / 36

Safed / 35

Vered Hagalil / 43

The Golan Heights / 21, 41, 62

Haifa / 34, 53

The Galil / 13, 15

Tiberias / 21

Zippori / 31

Lake Kinneret / 5, 57

Isfiya / 37

Nazareth, Nazerat Illit / 55

Zikhron Ya'acov / 24

Caesarea / 8

Uhm El Fahm / 59

Pardes Hanna / 24

Jenin / 51

Netanya / 8

Taiyiba, Tulkarm / 59

Herzliya / 8

Kiryat Shaul / 57

Tel Aviv / 6, 9, 10, 14, 15, 19,
23, 25, 28, 44, 50, 52, 57, 61

B'nei Brak / 54

Jericho / 30

Jaffa / 42

Ramla / 2, 3

Latrun, Sha'ar Hagai / 7

Rehovot / 28

Jerusalem / 1, 9, 16, 27, 32, 45, 47, 50

Ashdod / 49

Beit Shemesh / 7

Ashkelon / 60

Gaza / 60

Hebron / 26

Ein Gedi / 40, 57

Masada / 40

Beersheva / 29

Haluza / 11

Sodom / 56

Dimona / 6

Sde' Boker / 17

Hatseva / 22

Mitzpe Ramon / 38

Hai Bar / 33

Timna / 33

Eilat / 4, 12

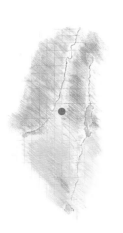

On Wednesday, May 4, 1994—only hours before more than 60 *Day in the Life* photographers set out to chronicle life across the State of Israel—Israel's prime minister, Yitzhak Rabin, and Yasser Arafat, chairman of the Palestine Liberation Organization, signed a peace agreement granting Palestinians in Gaza and Jericho limited self-rule.

On the following day, May 5, *Day in the Life* photographer Nik Wheeler went to the Erez checkpoint between Gaza and Israel. There, Israeli soldiers electronically scanned the identity cards of more than 10,000 Gazans who come to work in Israel each day. One irony of Israel's 27-year control of Gaza and the West Bank is that Palestinians and Israelis have become economically co-dependent. More than 20,000 Palestinians find their livelihood working for Israeli companies, while Israeli agriculture and construction rely, to some extent, on Palestinian labor.

NIK WHEELER

Bus passengers leaving Gaza to visit relatives in Israeli prisons. They step off their coaches for a search and questioning by Israeli border guards.

NIK WHEELER

In the children's house at Kibbutz Tze'lim near the Negev town of Haluza. Since the first *kibbutzim* (collective agricultural communities) were established in the early 1900s, these houses have been a hallmark of the communities' unique child-rearing practices. Traditionally, from birth until age 18, kibbutz children lived, not in their parents' homes, but with their peers in a separate house. Children visited their parents on weekends and in the afternoons, returning to the children's house to sleep. On many kibbutzim such as Tze'lim, however, these and other traditional practices have changed. At Tze'lim, children now spend their days at the children's house but return to their parents' homes at night.

BARBARA DEMOULIN

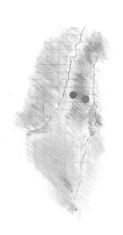

● **ABOVE**

At an Israeli army training base for women, young officer candidates clean their weapons and prepare for morning inspection. Nearly all Jewish Israelis are drafted at age 18. Unlike men, however, women serve for nearly two years instead of three and are barred from active combat duty.

SHLOMO ARAD

● **RIGHT**

A worshipper prays before the *bimah* in a Breslever synagogue in Jerusalem's Orthodox Mea Shearim section. Male congregants customarily wear a *tallit*, a fringed, four-cornered prayer shawl, and bind *tefillin*—black boxes containing four paragraphs from the Torah—to their hands and foreheads. Tefillin are worn to fulfill the Biblical instruction found in Deuteronomy 6:8: "You shall bind them as a sign on your hand and as frontlets between your eyes."

DANIEL LAINÉ

● **LEFT**

Yitzhak Rabin, Israel's prime minister and minister of defense, studies the morning news over a quick breakfast of grapefruit and coffee in the kitchen of his Tel Aviv home. Rabin spent the previous day in Cairo, where he signed a groundbreaking peace accord with Yasser Arafat, chairman of the Palestine Liberation Organization.

DAVID RUBINGER

● **ABOVE**

A customer at Cafe Tamar on Tel Aviv's bohemian Sheinkin Street catches up on the dramatic news of the recent autonomy accord.

MICHAL HEIMAN

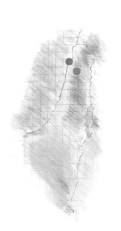

● **ABOVE**

Before leaving for work at his computer company in Haifa, Edwin Slonim enjoys a cuddle with his one-year-old son, Ilan, youngest of five children.

JEFFERY ALLAN SALTER

● **RIGHT**

In the village of Uhm El Fahm, southeast of Haifa, an Israeli Arab presses garments in a textile factory. Israeli Arabs—Moslem and Christian—remaining in Israel after the 1948 War of Independence have full rights as Israeli citizens, although they are exempt from military service. In the decades since Israel was established, the economic condition of Israeli Arabs has generally improved. Many have left traditional agricultural work for urban jobs in industry, trades and services.

SCOTT THODE

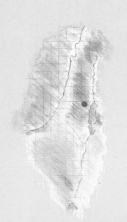

A Day in the Life of Mea Shearim Yeshivot

BY ALON REININGER

P hotographer Alon Reininger spent May 5 in the narrow streets of Mea Shearim, an ultra-Orthodox section of Jerusalem that maintains the old traditions and religious lifestyle of the Eastern European *shtetls*.

The heart of Mea Shearim—and all *haredi* (literally, God-fearing) communities—are the *yeshivot*, religious schools where students study and discuss the Torah, the Talmud and the religious commentary of the sages.

From the age of four until several years after they marry, and sometimes throughout their adult lives, many male haredim spend long hours each day learning, studying and debating holy texts. The academic method—based on chanting and noisy argument in pairs—has remained unchanged for centuries.

Enrollment in Israel's yeshivot has grown explosively over the past two generations. In all of Eastern Europe before the Holocaust, there were at most 35,000 yeshiva students. Today, in Israel alone there are nearly 50,000. This is due to government grants to yeshiva students, the very high birth rate of haredi families and, of course, to tradition. The high value that the community places on religious study means a haredi father almost always prefers to marry his daughter to a scholar.

● LEFT

F our-year-old students struggle to stay alert after a long day at the Torah Ve'Yirah Yeshiva in Mea Shearim.

● ABOVE

T wo haredi boys listen intently to their teacher's lessons. Yeshivot foster a lifelong devotion to learning Torah—a *mitzvah* (the fulfilling of a commandment) which weighs "as much as all the other *mitzvot* together," according to the Talmud.

Boys rush out to play during a break between study sessions at their Talmud Torah.

A rabbi dishes out lunch to *yeshiva bucherim* (yeshiva boys) at a Talmud Torah in Mea Shearim.

A pupil gathers the holy books at Yeshiva Torah Ve'Yirah before school lets out for the day. The school is run by the Netorei Karta, an extreme sect that refuses to recognize the existence of the State of Israel.

In the traditional method for learning Torah and Talmud, students at Yeshiva Torah Ve'Yirah repeat Hebrew and Yiddish words and phrases chanted by their teacher.

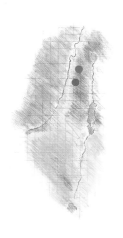

● **LEFT**

In Pardes Hanna, a town of vineyards and orange groves at the foot of the Carmel Mountains, artist Asnat Halter crafts ceramic designs.
ROBERT HOLMES

● **ABOVE**

Wheels of Kechkerval cheese made of sheep's milk are brushed and set out to dry on racks at the Shomron Dairy in Binyamina.
ROBERT HOLMES

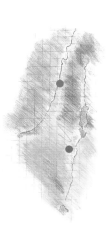

● RIGHT

Vi Lay, a seasonal worker from Thailand, harvests bunches of Japanese lemon flowers. These flowers are grown on the Hatseva *moshav*, a cooperative farming community in the parched Arava Valley south of the Dead Sea near the Jordanian border. Grown year-round in desert greenhouses, flowers account for a quarter of Israel's agricultural exports.

ACEY HARPER

● FOLLOWING PAGES

Turkeys flock in the poultry pens of Givat Hayim kibbutz outside Netanya. More than 2,000 turkeys are raised on the kibbutz, which also manufactures orange juice. Turkey and chicken are staples in Israel, where poultry consumption per capita is among the highest in the world.

RICK BROWNE

● LEFT

Cows graze lazily at Kibbutz Merom Golan near the Syrian border. The quiet pastoral scene belies the fact that the future of the Golan—specifically the possibility that the region may be returned to Syria—is a burning issue in Israel.

MEMO ZACK

● FOLLOWING PAGES

The Wanus family harvests bales of hay in El Ghazar, an Arab village near the Syrian and Lebanese borders in the Golan. Before the Six-Day War in 1967, El Ghazar was part of Syria. After Syria retreated, the town was nationless for three months, until Israeli troops moved in and claimed it.

RAZI

Tel Aviv's streets teem with thousands of boxy apartment buildings and an increasing number of modern high-rises, many built within the past 25 years. When it was founded on the empty sand dunes north of Jaffa by Zionists in 1909, Tel Aviv was the first new Jewish town established in Palestine in 2,000 years. Since then, as the highly regarded Israeli architect Ariyeh Sharon once remarked, Tel Aviv "just growed."

PAUL CHESLEY

A Day on the Streets of Nazareth and Nazerat Illit

BY JOEL SARTORE

Myth and reality on the main road to Nazerat Illit.

A television in a repair shop broadcasts news of Israel's historic peace accord with the PLO, while outside, tourists hunt for bargains in the Arab market.

Shoppers in the winding old market area.

At a housing center for Russian immigrants in the new Jewish development of Nazerat Illit. The women chat while Kajin Moshe—formerly director of a university science department in Russia—surveys the passing scene.

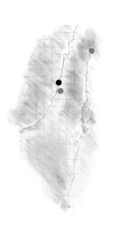

Israeli soldiers in the Golan Heights test their gas masks by entering a tent filled with a foul chemical odor. If a soldier can detect the smell—called *bananit* because of its unmistakable stink of rotten bananas—the gas mask needs repairs.

LORI GRINKER

In a clean room at the Weizmann Institute of Science in Rehovot, south of Tel Aviv, Dr. Vladimir Umansky grows thin layers of semiconductor crystals. Named for Israel's first president—the Russian-born chemist Chaim Weizmann—the Weizmann Institute is a world-renowned scientific research center. Recently, the Institute has benefited from an influx of talented Russian scientists such as Dr. Umansky.

DOUGLAS KIRKLAND

A civilian worker repairs a tank in an Israeli defense plant near Tel Aviv. This task is sometimes performed by Jewish volunteers from around the world.

YOSSI COHEN

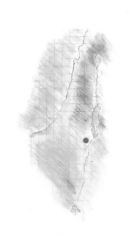

● **LEFT**

In Sodom (S'dom)—near the spot where, according to Scripture, Lot's wife was turned into a pillar of salt—the Dead Sea Works harvests a mineral bonanza from the salt-rich sea, including vast quantities of potash, bromine and magnesium chloride.

MOSHE SHAI

● **ABOVE**

Drivers share a smoke before heading off with their load of chemicals from the Dead Sea Works factory.

MOSHE SHAI

● **LEFT**

The Pil tobacco factory in Rosh-Ha'Ayin, near Tel Aviv. Per capita, Israelis and Palestinians are among the biggest consumers of cigarettes in the world.

ELDAD RAFAELI

● **ABOVE**

A salon owner scans the busy pedestrian scene on Jerusalem's trendy Ben Yehuda Street.

PAUL CHESLEY

Abraham Shmulevich, armed with an Uzi submachine gun, takes two-year-old Simcha grocery shopping in Kiryat Arba, outside the West Bank city of Hebron. Shmulevich, a Russian who made his *aliyah* (immigration to Israel) in 1991, lives in Beit Hadassah, a small enclave of Jewish families in central Hebron.

As the burial site of the Biblical patriarchs Abraham, Isaac and Jacob, Hebron is sacred to religious Jews and Moslems alike. After Israel captured the city from Jordan during the Six-Day War, the Israeli government refused to allow Jews to settle in Hebron, fearing Arab reprisals. Settlers, however, were allowed to build a new settlement, Kiryat Arba, at the edge of town. In 1979, a group of Jewish women and children seized the former Beit Hadassah complex and refused to leave. The group finally won permission to live there, now one of four small Jewish settlements in Hebron.

ED KASHI

A horse breeder puts his steed through its paces in the Upper Galilee's Beit Netofa Valley.

AVI GANOR

● **LEFT**

This church in Capernaum overlooks the Sea of Galilee (Lake Kinneret) where Jesus Christ began his ministry and where Peter, his apostle, was born. It was on a hilltop near here that Jesus proclaimed, "Blessed are the meek, for they shall inherit the earth."
LARRY PRICE

● **FOLLOWING PAGES**

The still, salty waters of the Dead Sea are not technically dead—11 varieties of bacteria somehow survive the inhospitable depths—but they support no fish or other forms of marine life. Due to evaporation and diversion of water from the Jordan River by both Israel and Jordan, the Dead Sea is shrinking at an alarming rate. Ambitious, hugely expensive (and some say farfetched) pipeline projects to bring in supplementary water from the Mediterranean or the Red Sea have been under discussion for years.
CLAUS MEYER

● **LEFT**

Itzhak Maoz is raising his two sons, Ran, 8, and Shai, 15, near the Jordanian border on the Hatseva moshav. Like the more well-known kibbutz, a moshav is primarily an agricultural settlement. On a kibbutz. work and property are shared communally. On a moshav, families run their own households, farm their own land but conduct marketing and purchasing collectively.

ACEY HARPER

● **ABOVE**

Koram Halter, 5, cuddles her 10-day-old kittens in the garden of her home in Pardes Hanna.

ROBERT HOLMES

DAY IN THE LIFE PORTRAITS
BY RAZI

● A 14-year-old hockey player at the Beit Canada sports center in Metulla, near the Lebanese border. The center was built with the help of donations from Canada's Jewish community.

● In El Ghazar, Gara Salman, 15, poses with her little brother in her bedroom, which she has decorated with photographs of her favorite singers and movie stars.

● Hedva Abscar, 22, from Lod, traveled to Kiryat Shemona to attend a wedding.

● Nabeha Salman in the living room of her home in El Ghazar.

● **LEFT**

The fifteen-year-old Gol twins hold copies of the Talmud, a compendium of Jewish law and tradition, at a Lubavitcher synagogue in Nazerat Illit.

JOEL SARTORE

● **ABOVE**

Aida Abublaya, a Bedouin shepherdess, lives with her husband's family at Wadi Nafikh, near Beersheva.

NINA BARNETT

A Day in the Life from Above

BY DUBY TAL, ISRAEL'S FOREMOST AERIAL PHOTOGRAPHER

● **ABOVE:** Riders race across the sand on the spectacular Mediterranean beaches of Ga'ash between Herzliya and Netanya.

● **PREVIOUS PAGES:** The Mediterranean surf pounds the beaches near Netanya, a resort community, retirement area and the hub of Israel's formidable diamond industry.

● **ABOVE:** Off the Bat Galim promenade in Haifa. Mount Carmel is in the background.

● **RIGHT:** The ruins of King Herod's Masada palace sit atop a remote, 1,300-ft. rock in the Judean Desert. Masada was seized by Jewish zealots in 66 CE. After a long siege, 960 men, women and children took their own lives rather than face capture by the Romans.

● B'nei Brak: Hat shops are fixtures in Orthodox communities, where devout Jews cover their heads as an act of piety. **EMMANUEL SANTOS**

● In Kiryat Shaul cemetery, a worker seals a grave with a marble slab. **RUSSELL SACKS**

● Near the West Bank town of Jenin, villagers make charcoal for nearby businesses. **RUSSELL SACKS**

● In the streets of Safed (S'fat), a center of Judaic art and mysticism in the Upper Galilee. **ALEX LEVAC**

● RIGHT

Accompanied by armed chaperones, schoolchildren from Ein Gev, on the eastern shore of Lake Kinneret, go on a spring hike along the Jordan River.

MICHA BAR'AM

● **LEFT**

Before statehood, Zionist women guarded Jewish settlements and served in underground military organizations. During the War of Independence, they fought side-by-side with men in the newly established Israel Defense Forces (IDF). Today, most 18-year-old Israeli women are drafted along with men into the IDF, where they serve actively for nearly two years and remain on reserve until the age of 24. Although female soldiers are not permitted on active combat missions, they perform a wide range of duties and have been particularly successful as instructors. The Israeli army has found that young men learn tank maneuvers, weapons-handling and marksmanship better and more quickly from young women than they do from older men. Here, an instructor teaches a trainee sniper techniques.

NINA BARNETT

● **ABOVE, TOP**

Riflery instructors take an *al fresco* lunch break.

NINA BARNETT

● **ABOVE**

In Israel, the armed forces are the great melting-pot. Here, soldier Chanita Reuven gives Hebrew language lessons to Ethiopian draftees near Karmiel.

GERD LUDWIG

● **ABOVE**

At the Sisters of St. Joseph's home for aged nuns in Jaffa, the Mother Superior, Sister Raphael Mikhail, lends a hand in the kitchen, ladling out soup for the communal meal. Nuns from France, Germany, Belgium, Switzerland and Ireland retire to this well-tended convent in the Holy Land.

SYLVIA PLACHY

● **RIGHT**

In the Orthodox community of B'nei Brak, needy residents come to the community kitchen of Beit Tamhooy for a free hot meal.

EMMANUEL SANTOS

● **LEFT**

Young haredi students share a
hot lunch in the dining room
of Etz Haim Yeshiva in Jerusalem's
Orthodox Mea Shearim community.
DANIEL LAINÉ

● **ABOVE**

A sweet snack at an outdoor cafe
on Ben Yehuda Street in
Jerusalem's New City.
PAUL CHESLEY

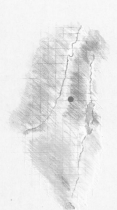

A Day in the Life of Neve Tirtza
Women's Prison

BY JANE EVELYN ATWOOD

Photographer Jane Evelyn Atwood recorded a typical day at
Neve Tirtza Prison in Ramla, southeast of Tel Aviv. Most of
the 119 inmates are convicted of drug-related crimes. Nearly all
are Jewish, as Arab women have been incarcerated in a separate
facility since the 1980s.

Atwood, who has photographed in women's prisons around the
world, was surprised by the "soft," relaxed atmosphere of Neve
Tirtza. Prisoners were allowed access to television and newspapers. Women with a record of good behavior were permitted to
leave the prison grounds on 24- or 48-hour passes. And inmates
with babies were allowed to keep their children with them until
the age of two.

As in all of the women's prisons she has visited, Atwood was
struck by the painful stories told by many of the inmates. "One
woman was jailed after stealing food to feed her children. Her cell
is full of bags of *matzot*, cheese and other food that she hoards
because she is always frightened that she won't get enough."

● **LEFT**

While she awaits sentencing, a
prisoner in Neve Tirtza gets
a light from another inmate through
the cell bars.

● **ABOVE**

A woman confined to isolation
stares through the slot in her
cell door. Prisoners are quarantined
in Neve Tirtza's isolation section for
such offenses as fighting or attempt-
ing to escape.

Geulah Harel (left), the director of Neve Tirtza, in her office with assistant director, Dalia Nir. Only female corrections officers work in Neve Tirtza Prison. Unlike most women's prisons Atwood has visited, the officers of Neve Tirtza are considered compassionate by the inmates.

An inmate who has received a 48-hour pass to leave the prison is searched by a corrections officer for drugs and other contraband. Prisoners must demonstrate consistently good behavior and complete a quarter of their sentence to earn these furloughs.

In the courtyard of Section C, where privileged inmates enjoy a garden, Rabbi F. Jacobs counsels a prisoner. A former Vermont resident, the prison rabbi advises women on family matters and provides religious instruction at Neve Tirtza and two other penitentiaries.

At Neve Tirtza, prisoners with babies are given special cells with access to a nursery. "The babies are pampered and played with and adored by all the other prisoners," Atwood says. After they reach the age of two, the children are placed in the care of a family member or a foster home or are sent to live on a kibbutz.

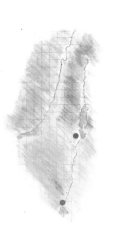

● **ABOVE**

On a Dead Sea beach outside the Moriah Plaza Hotel in Newe Zohar.

MOSHE SHAI

● **LEFT**

A puffed-up, yellow-spotted burrfish bobs in the blue waters of the Red Sea, a favorite diving spot for scuba enthusiasts.

DAVID DOUBILET

● **RIGHT**

Maya Zilber, chief curator of the Dolphin Reef Center in Eilat, takes a dive with a dolphin. Zilber and other specialists train the dolphins, which were brought to the Red Sea from Russia and Japan. For a fee, tourists can don underwater gear, swim with the animals and assist with their care and feeding.

DAVID DOUBILET

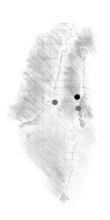

Tourists bake in the sun under a crust of Dead Sea mud, thought by many to be therapeutic. Israel's *Yam Hamelah* (Sea of Salt) is the lowest point on earth, more than 1,300 feet (400 meters) below sea level. As a result of evaporation and water diversion, the sea contains 10 to 20 times the ocean's concentration of magnesium, iodine and bromine. The alleged curative powers of its water, mud and sulfur springs have made the Dead Sea a popular resort for vacationers suffering from arthritis, rheumatism and skin diseases.

CLAUS MEYER

● **ABOVE**

Outside a music store in Ashdod, a major industrial port south of Tel Aviv.

STEVE RUBIN

● **ABOVE**

At the Haas Promenade, a recently constructed scenic vantage point overlooking Jerusalem.

RAGHU RAI

● **FOLLOWING PAGES**

A souvenir vendor exhibits his olive wood wares on the Mount of Olives in Jerusalem.

RAGHU RAI

On the roof of Jerusalem's Church of the Holy Sepulcher, built above the rock where Christ is said to have been crucified, stands a cluster of simple dwellings. These cell-like huts are inhabited by Jerusalem's Ethiopian monks who were banished to the roof by their rivals, the Coptic Christians, in one of many—often bloody—disputes over control of the basilica.

Despite their current exile to the roof, the Ethiopians claim unique, pre-Christian links to the city of Jerusalem. The emperors of Ethiopia, known as the "Lions of Judah," maintained that they were descended from Menelik I, son of King Solomon and the queen of Sheba. Today, some 100 Ethiopian monks and nuns live on the rooftop Ethiopian Monastery and in a century-old compound, called Mount Paradise, in West Jerusalem. At left, an Ethiopian nun and child visit the roof of the Holy Sepulcher.

CRISTINA GARCIA RODERO

A DAY IN THE LIFE OF THE WESTERN WALL

The Western Wall, sometimes called "The Wailing Wall," is the holiest place in Judaism. The last remaining section of the rampart which encircled the Temple Court in ancient times, it was built by Herod the Great in 20 BCE. Held by Jordan from 1948 to 1967, the Western Wall was captured by Israeli paratroopers at the climax of the Six-Day War in 1967. Immediately after the war, the plaza in front of the site was cleared, and 200,000 Israeli Jews traveled to Jerusalem to touch the Wall's sacred stones.

Thirteen-year-old boys enter adulthood in boisterous Bar Mitzvah ceremonies at the Wall. In accordance with Orthodox tradition, their mothers and sisters watch from a segregated women's section. **RAGHU RAI**

Black-garbed haredim assemble for prayer. **ROBERT HOLMES**

Guns and prayer books stand ready for Israeli troops who will swear their oath of military allegiance by the Wall. **PAUL CHESLEY**

A worshipper peers through the *mechitsah*, the partition that separates the men's and women's sections of the plaza. Orthodox tradition requires the separation of the sexes during prayer in order to minimize distractions. **PAUL CHESLEY**

● ABOVE

An Israeli soldier drapes his head with a tallit and bows in prayer before the Western Wall. Paratroopers are sworn in at the Wall to commemorate their role in the capture of the site from Jordan in 1967.

PAUL CHESLEY

▶ RIGHT

Jerusalem's gleaming Dome of the Rock, built in the 7th century by Caliph Abd el-Malik, encloses a huge rock imbued with religious significance. It is here that Abraham is said to have offered his son Isaac for sacrifice. Moslems believe that Abraham intended to sacrifice Ishmael, father of the Arabs, here, and that it was from this rock that Mohammed ascended to heaven.

Once sheathed in pure gold, the dome of the third holiest shrine in Islam has since been covered in dull lead and, more recently, in gold-colored aluminum. In 1994, however, a new $8 million dome was completed, coated with 176 pounds of 24 carat gold—a gift from King Hussein of Jordan.

NICK KELSH

Haredi children celebrate a joyful family Bar Mitzvah at the Western Wall.

PAUL CHESLEY

Israeli fashion designer Dorin Frankfurt, whose collections have drawn praise in New York and London, looks out over the streets of Old Jaffa.

MICHAL HEIMAN

● ABOVE AND LEFT

Ben Yehuda Street, a popular pedestrian mall in the New City of Jerusalem, draws young, chic Jerusalemites with its stylish boutiques, cafes and impromptu street performances.

PAUL CHESLEY

On Ben Yehuda Street in Jerusalem's New City.

PAUL CHESLEY

On Moshav Givat Yeshayahu, Meiri Levy relaxes with two-year-old Neta, after his day's work in the vineyards is done. Levy, a former Israeli air force pilot, left the military to raise grapes and chickens with 60 other families in the Beit Shemesh Valley.

NINA BARNETT

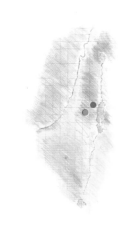

AN ANXIOUS DAY AT HADASSAH HOSPITAL

BY NICK KELSH

Alison Nasser hugs ISAC volunteer Aliza Nesher with thanks and relief, after Nesher arrives with donated funds for her baby's surgery.

Hadassah Hospital—founded in 1913 to care for all patients regardless of their religion or means—is now one of the world's most advanced medical centers. In the crowded pediatric ward, photographer Nick Kelsh found Alison Nasser and her two-week-old daughter, Nadine. Nasser, an American immigrant married to a Palestinian, was waiting anxiously for her baby to be admitted for surgery to correct a malfunctioning heart valve. Compounding their anguish, Nasser and her husband did not have the money to pay for the life-saving procedure.

Shortly before the baby was scheduled to go into the operating room, Aliza Nesher, a volunteer from a Jerusalem charity group, the Intercongregational Social Assistance Center (ISAC), suddenly appeared with donated funds to pay for Nadine's medical care. Soon after, another miracle occurred: Nadine's heart valve spontaneously started working normally. Doctors told Nasser that surgery was unnecessary. She and her baby could go home.

ABOVE: While Nasser tells her husband that their baby's heart valve has suddenly started working, a nurse interrupts her to say the baby can check out of the hospital and go home.

LEFT: In Jerusalem's Hadassah Hospital, Alison Nasser holds her infant, Nadine, while they await life-saving surgery to repair the baby's heart valve.

The walls of Akko were built by the Turks atop the ruins of the vast, largely unexcavated 13th century capital of the Christian Crusaders. One of the world's oldest towns, Akko was a port prized by Alexander the Great, Pompey, Saladin and Richard the Lionhearted. In 1799, Napoleon tried and failed to conquer Akko, claiming that had he been successful, "the world would have been mine."

RICK RICKMAN

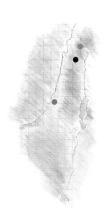

Potato growers at Brur Chail near
Ashkelon check the crop they
planted for McDonald's expanding
fast-food business in Israel. In
February 1994, McDonald's escalated
Israel's burger wars with a 500-seat
restaurant near Tel Aviv. Crowds
waited for up to two hours for Big
Macs and McNuggets. McDonald's
faces competition from the local
Burger Ranch chain and from a group
of burger stands called McDavid's.

NIK WHEELER

In Kfar Yuval, a settlement of Jews
from India located near the
Lebanese border, Nehemya Tiferet
tends the 1,800 chickens he raises
with his wife, Rivka.

LORI GRINKER

A worker hoses down hogs at the
Mizra pig farm in Zippori, near
Nazareth. Owned by two Jewish
brothers, the Mizra farm raises 2,500
animals. Although the eating of pork
is banned by both Jewish and
Moslem dietary laws, pork is popular
among Israeli Christians and some
secular Jews, especially the large wave
of recent Russian immigrants. In an
effort to court the ultra-Orthodox
Agudat Yisrael Party, the Likud-led
government threatened to ban pig
breeding and the sale of pork
products in Israel in 1990. Angry
non-kosher butchers responded by
handing out ham sandwiches in the
streets of downtown Jerusalem. The
measure never passed.

HIROJI KUBOTA

Ajogger on the beach at Herzliya, north of Tel Aviv. Founded in 1924 as an agricultural community, Herzliya was named for Theodore Herzl, the liberal, secularist founder of the Zionist movement. Herzliya's beautiful beaches, luxury hotels and high-priced homes make it one of Israel's most exclusive areas. It may also be one of the most open-minded, offering a nude beach—one of the very few in Israel—as well as a separate beach for heavily clad religious bathers.

RICK BROWNE

In the Negev Desert, farmer Davis Shahak skims his red ultralight over the date groves of the Hatseva moshav.

ACEY HARPER

Ilan Dvir rounds up alpacas he brought from Chile to his ranch near Mitzpe Ramon in the Negev Desert. Dvir's original herd of 175 alpacas arrived by plane in 1990. In their new Israeli home—the only alpaca ranch outside the Americas— the animals are raised for their fine, soft wool, which is spun and woven on the ranch. The Dvirs, whose herd now numbers 300, earn half their income from selling alpaca wool to places as far away as Japan and half from tourists who visit the ranch.

JAMES MARSHALL

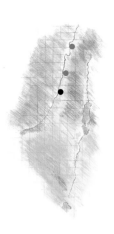

● **PRECEDING PAGES**

A wine maker peers out of the fermentation tank he is inspecting at the Baron Cellars winery in the heart of Shomron, Israel's largest grape-growing region. Baron Cellars was established a decade ago by Jonathan Tishbi, a fifth-generation vintner. Named for the Baron de Rothschild, who founded Israel's modern wine industry, the Baron winery produces 30,000 cases each year of fine kosher cabernet sauvignons, chardonnays, sauvignon blancs and rieslings, which it sells to customers ranging from El Al airlines to Buckingham Palace.

ROBERT HOLMES

● **ABOVE**

Jewish and Arab shopkeepers, laborers and fishermen gather regularly in this coffeehouse in Akko for high-pressure games of dominoes and poker.

RICK RICKMAN

May 5 was a quiet trading day on the Tel Aviv stock exchange, despite the fact that Israel signed a precedent-setting peace accord with the PLO the day before. Since 1992, when the government liberalized its economic policies, Israel's stock exchange has seen dynamic activity in both the blue-chip Mishtanim stock index and the Karam index of small firms.

C. W. GRIFFIN

THE FIRST DAY OF A NEW LIFE IN ISRAEL

BY MARINA YURCHENKO

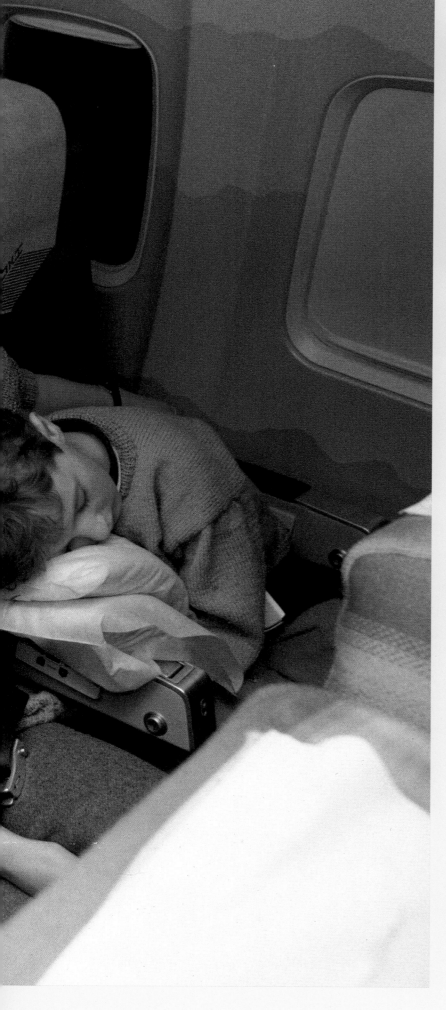

Marina Yurchenko's long day in the life of Israel began at 2:00AM, when she raced to Moscow's international airport just in time to board a plane to Israel. Her last-minute assignment: to travel with several families leaving Russia for new homes and lives in Israel—part of the flood of half a million immigrants who have arrived from the former Soviet Union since 1989.

"The families were very subdued," Yurchenko says. "But they were excited about moving to Israel and seeing their close relatives who had immigrated earlier." Yurchenko chronicled the flight and the joyous welcome the passengers received when they landed at Ben Gurion Airport. She then accompanied the Russian families home, where they unpacked and began their new lives near Tel Aviv.

Israel's Law of Return provides that Jews anywhere in the world have the unassailable right to immigrate to Israel, and world Jewry has given millions of dollars to relocate Russian Jews to Israel since the fall of communism.

● **LEFT**

After leaving their home in Nizhni Novgorod, Alexander Sokol, a pianist, and his wife, Irina, an English teacher, sit quietly while their eight-year-old son sleeps on the long plane trip to a new life in Israel.

● **ABOVE**

When the Sokols arrive at Ben Gurion Airport, they are greeted by Alexander's family, who immigrated to Israel earlier.

Yaffa and Rosa Darmanuf (center), who immigrated to Israel from the town of Machatzkala in Dagastan, watch as the Sokols arrive at their new home.

Leonard Sokol helps his son unpack. He holds a poster for one of Alexander's piano concerts in Italy.

Alexander tries out his new piano, while Leonard catches up with his grandson, Dima.

Two months before Alexander Sokol arrived in Israel with his family, his father, Leonard, immigrated with his wife, Sima, from the Ukraine.

● **ABOVE**

The grave of Oskar Schindler—
a member of the Nazi Party who
saved the lives of 1,200 Jews during
World War II—lies in the Roman
Catholic cemetery on Jerusalem's
Mount Zion. Schindler's story is now
known worldwide as a result of
Thomas Keneally's best-selling book
and Stephen Spielberg's acclaimed
film, *Schindler's List*. From 1939 until the
end of the war, Schindler housed, fed
and employed Jews in his enamelware
and munitions factory in Krakow,
spending his fortune to keep them out
of the Nazi death camps. Beginning in
the 1960s, Schindler visited Israel
annually as the guest of his former
employees, whom he always called his
"children." After his death in Frankfurt
in 1974, Schindler's body was buried
in Jerusalem, according to his request.

NUBAR ALEXANIAN

● **RIGHT**

At Yad Vashem, the memorial to
the Holocaust on Jerusalem's
Mount of Remembrance. Robert
Bos helps his eight-year-old son,
Lenny, place a stone—an act of
bearing witness, according to Jewish
tradition—on Nador Gild's sculp-
ture, *Memorial to the Victims of the Death
Camps*. Bos, a native of the Netherlands, came to Yad Vashem for the
first time because his young children
wanted to understand why so many
of their relatives had perished during
World War II.

Yad Vashem's Avenue of the
Righteous Gentiles is a lane lined
with 6,000 trees named for non-Jews
who heroically saved Jews during the
Holocaust. There, Bos discovered a
tree planted in honor of Jante
Wissema—the woman who saved
his father's life by hiding him from
the Nazis in her village in northern
Holland.

NICK KELSH

127

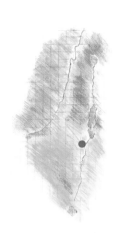

● LEFT
Naomi Becker field-strips and cleans the family's Uzi submachine gun while her four boys watch a videotape with friends. Hatseva moshav is near the Jordanian border, and members of the moshav cooperate with the military in local security efforts.

ACEY HARPER

In the West Bank town of Jericho,
Israeli soldiers patrol streets where
demonstrators celebrate the signing
of the Palestinian autonomy accord.
MIKI KRATSMAN

● RIGHT

On the "Shouting Hill" outside the Golan Heights village of Majdal Shams, a Druze woman calls through a megaphone to her relatives across the border in Syria. Many Druze families were divided when Israel took the Golan Heights from Syria during the Six-Day War in 1967. Families regularly communicate across the border at the Shouting Hill.

MEMO ZACK

● FOLLOWING PAGES

Bedouin sell and barter sheep at a market in Beersheva, the largest city in the Negev Desert. The Bedouin have inhabited the Negev for thousands of years. Traditionally nomadic (though less so these days), Bedouin life revolves around their herds of sheep, goats and camels. These animals keep them well-supplied with milk and meat, as well as hair for weaving into tent cloth. Livestock are also sold or traded to procure television sets, refrigerators, pick-up trucks and other modern luxuries.

ANTONIN KRATOCHVIL

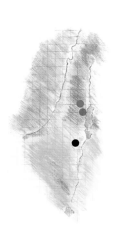

An Arizona tourist steadies
herself for a five-shekel camel
ride at Qalya, by the Dead Sea.
CLAUS MEYER

● **ABOVE**
In the narrow, winding streets of
the Old City's Moslem Quarter,
furniture delivery is decidedly
low-tech.
NUBAR ALEXANIAN

● **RIGHT**
In the Judean Desert, a Bedouin
businessman runs his tour
company from the saddle.
MOSHE SHAI

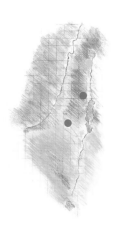

● **PREVIOUS PAGES**

A visitor to the tent of Muhammed Al Tory and his family in the Negev Desert near Beersheva. Like many Bedouin in the area, the Al Tory family actually resides in a conventional, permanent house behind the tent. However, the traditional *bayt al-sha'r* (literally, "house of hair"), made of animal-hair cloth, is still used by the men for conducting business and entertaining visitors.

ANTONIN KRATOCHVIL

● **ABOVE**

In Jerusalem's Armenian Quarter, Bishop Guregh Kapikian recites Armenian poetry with students graduating from the Holy Martyrs Armenian Day School. The Armenians' presence in Jerusalem dates back nearly 1,700 years to Armenia's conversion to Christianity in 301 CE.

NUBAR ALEXANIAN

● **RIGHT**

German pilgrims immerse themselves in the Jordan River at a baptismal site operated by Kibbutz Kinneret, one of the oldest kibbutzim in Israel.

MICHA BAR-AM

● **LEFT AND ABOVE**

Finished in 1969, the Basilica of the Annunciation was built over the site in Nazareth where the archangel Gabriel is said to have appeared before Mary to announce the coming birth of Christ. The lower level of the church incorporates remains of older Christian sanctuaries dating back to 356 CE. Nazareth's town planners are busy improving the city's religious shrines and facilities in preparation for the flood of Christian visitors expected for the 2,000th anniversary of Christ's birth.

JOEL SARTORE

A Quirky Day in the Life of Jaffa

BY SYLVIA PLACHY

ABOVE AND BELOW: In the Shouk Hapishpeshim, a huge street market filled with junk and treasure in old Jaffa.

ABOVE AND BELOW: In a Christian cemetery overlooking the Mediterranean Sea.

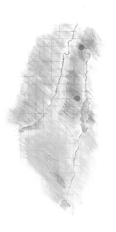

● **ABOVE**

Maronite men carry coffins they have brought from the village of Jish to their family tomb in Bar'am, near the Lebanese border. During the 1948 War of Independence, the Arab Christian Maronites were forced to abandon their homes in Bar'am and resettle in Jish, three miles (five kilometers) to the south. Today, Bar'am is an uninhabited village known for its 1,800-year-old synagogue, said to be the burial place of the Biblical Queen Esther. The Israeli Supreme Court has recently ruled that the 1,500 Maronite residents of Jish may return to Bar'am.

SUSAN MEISELAS

● ABOVE

Jews and Christians agree that the Last Judgment will take place when the Messiah raises the dead on Jerusalem's Mount of Olives and enters the Old City through the Golden Gate. Perhaps because of this, a burial plot in the Mount of Olives' Jewish Cemetery—an ancient necropolis—costs as much as $50,000. Once covered with shady olive groves, the Mount was stripped of its trees by the Romans, who used the wood for weapons to seize Jerusalem in 70 CE. For centuries, the Mount of Olives has drawn pilgrims and tourists to its tombs and holy sites, where Jesus "beheld the city, and wept over it" (Luke 19:41), and later, the Gospel says, ascended into heaven.

RAGHU RAI

● FOLLOWING PAGES

For religious Jews, it is a mitzvah to fulfill the biblical commandment, "Be fruitful and multiply." As a result, large families with seven to twelve children are the norm in the haredi communities of Israel. At a maternity home outside Jerusalem, the bassinets are bumper-to-bumper.

ALON REININGER

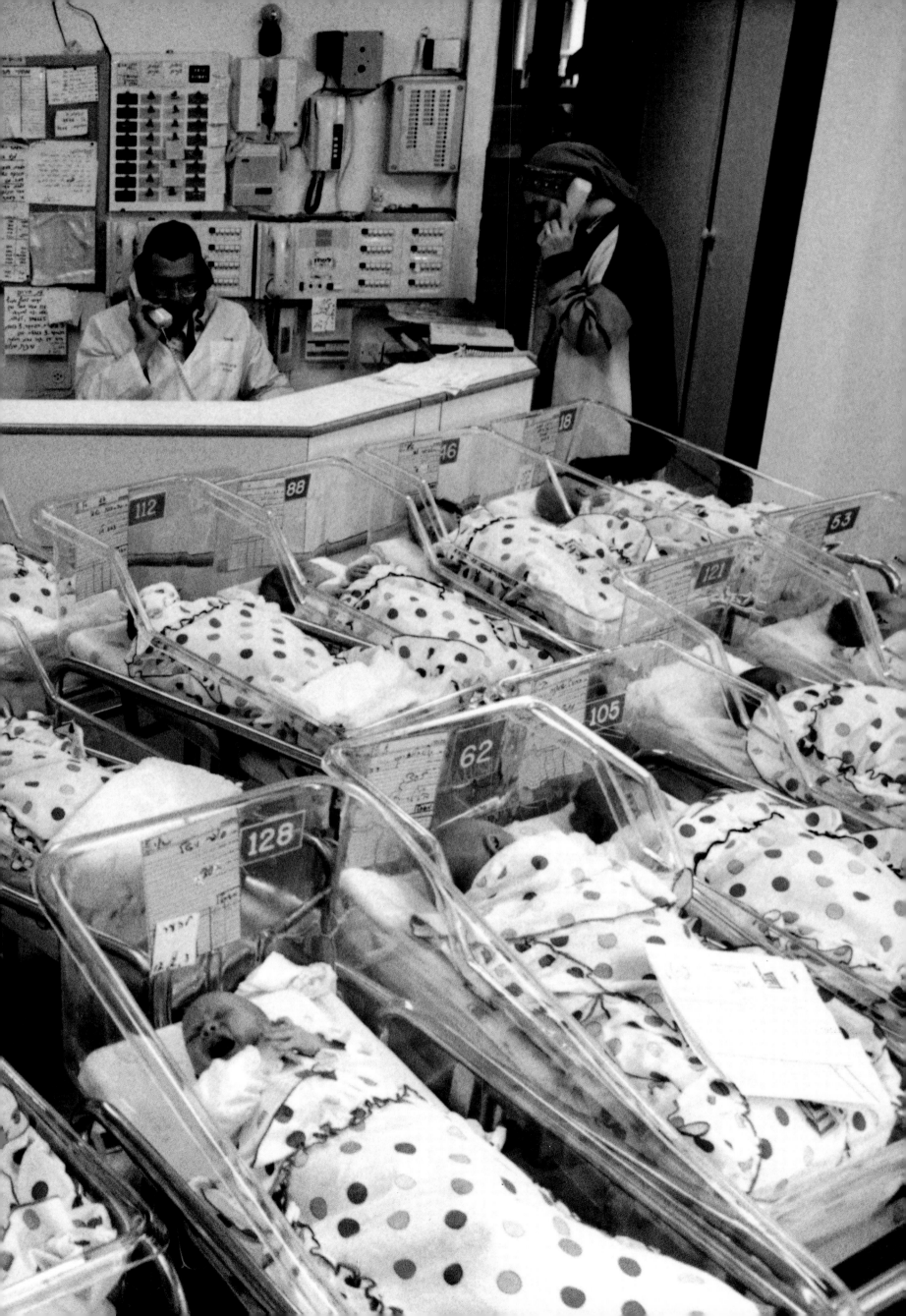

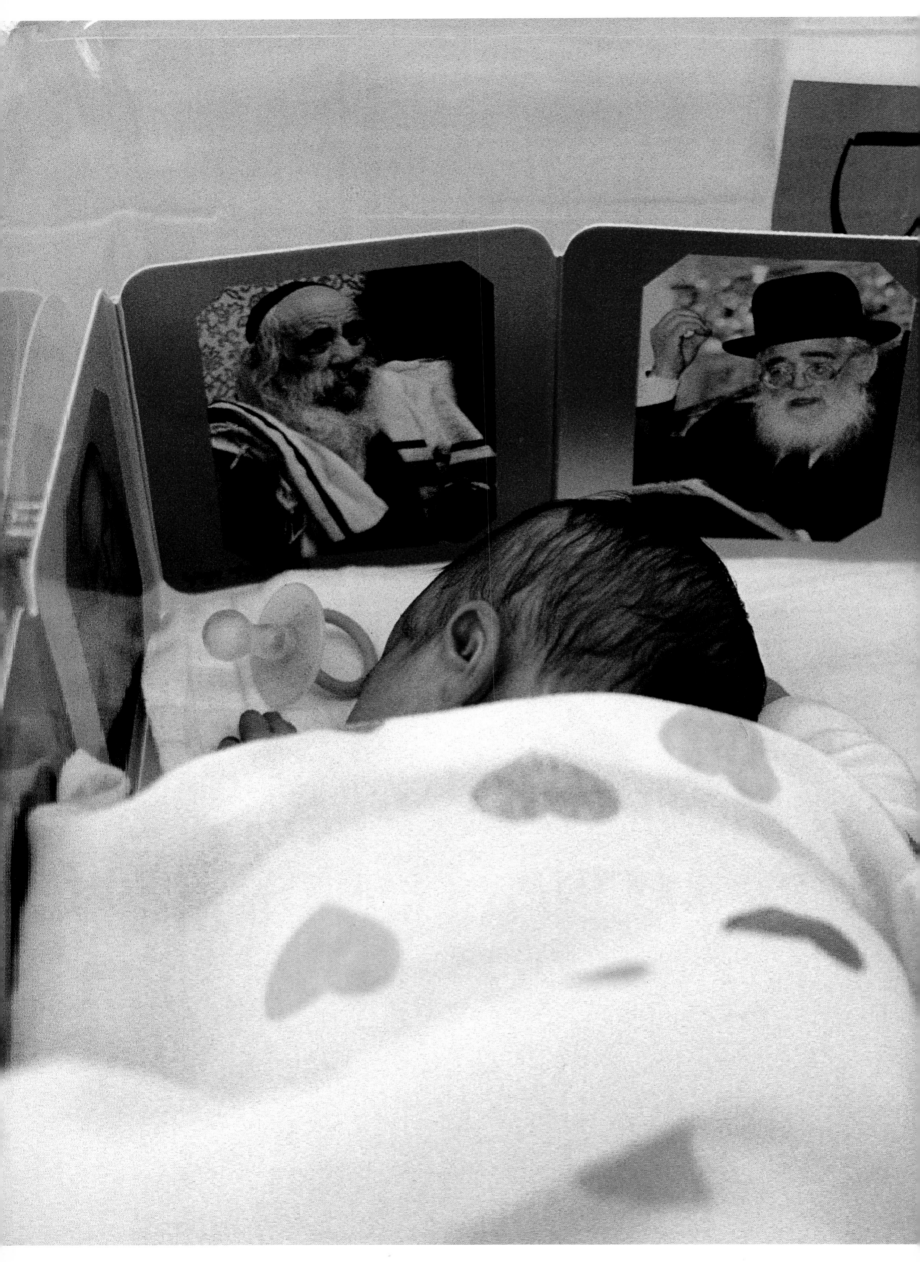

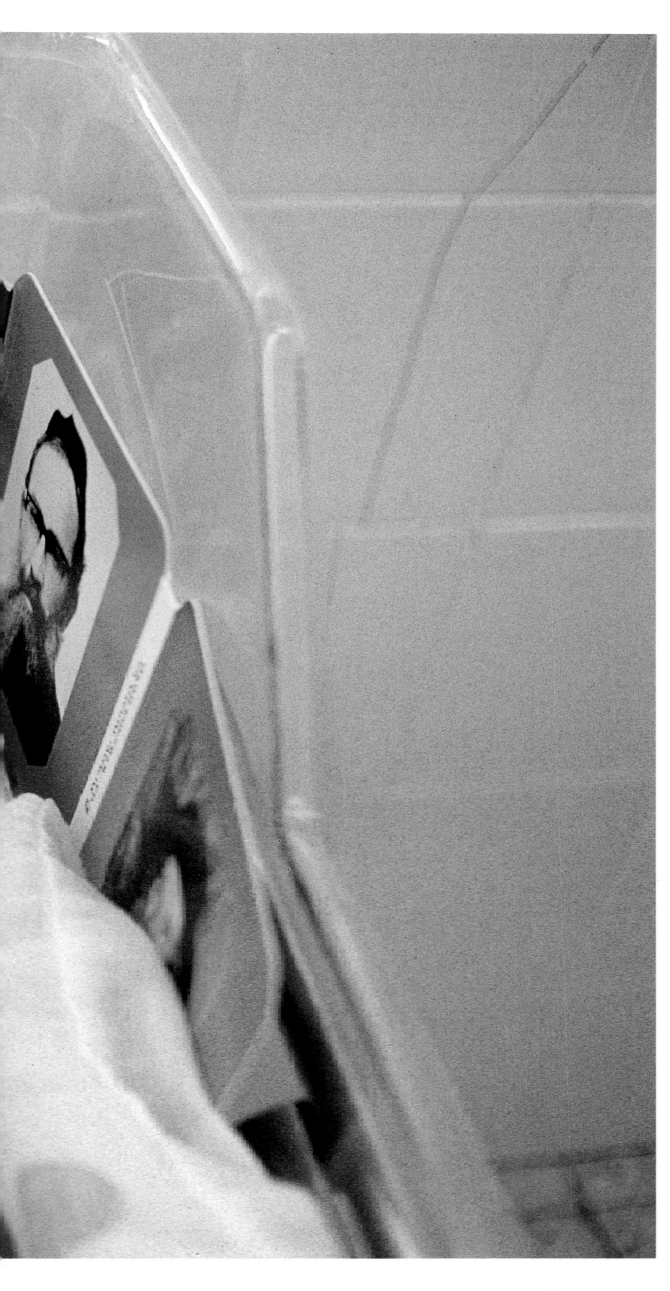

● **LEFT**

Early influences on a newborn at the maternity hospital in religious B'nei Brak.

EMMANUEL SANTOS

● LEFT

In the Druze village of Isfiya, near Haifa, family and friends gather in the home of Klil Saba to celebrate the circumcision of his first son. Although the Druze perform circumcision for health reasons rather than as a religious rite, many now celebrate the event with a party. This is probably due to their contact with Israeli Jews who joyously observe the traditional *brit milah*.

The 70,000 Israeli Druze speak Arabic and practice a secretive religion that broke from Islam 900 years ago. Druze practitioners believe in the transmigration of souls and hold that caliph al-Hakim bi'Amr Allah, who disappeared mysteriously in Egypt in 1021, is the messiah. The Druze carefully guard the secrets of their faith and have not accepted any converts since 1043. Despite the insular nature of their religion, the Druze have integrated successfully into Israeli society, serving in the armed forces, the border patrol and the Knesset.

PASCAL MAITRE

● FOLLOWING PAGES

This young Arab bride and groom celebrate their nuptials, Akko-style, by cruising the harbor in a red wedding boat bedecked with flowers, streamers and colorful crepe. The wedding ship is provided by a former fisherman who found a more profitable use for his skiff. The 19-year-old bride admitted to photographer Rick Rickman that she would have enjoyed her wedding more had she not been terrified of water.

RICK RICKMAN

THE FIRST DAY IN THE LIFE OF A MARRIAGE

BY CAROL GUZY, WINNER OF THE PULITZER PRIZE IN PHOTOGRAPHY

In Tiberias, on the western shore of Lake Kinneret, photographer Carol Guzy was invited to the wedding of Mayah Barda and Yariv Amzaleg, a huge, happy affair attended by hundreds of guests.

During the traditional Jewish ceremony, the bride was attended by two bridesmaids, including her admiring little sister Hilla Barda.

The newlyweds share a toast before the banquet begins.

Guests parade the bride around the room in a traditional dance of celebration.

On the crowded dance floor, guests dance to songs like Whitney Houston's "I Will Always Love You."

● **ABOVE AND RIGHT**

Aspiring young dancers receive instruction at the Rubin Academy in Jerusalem's Rehavia neighborhood.

PAUL CHESLEY

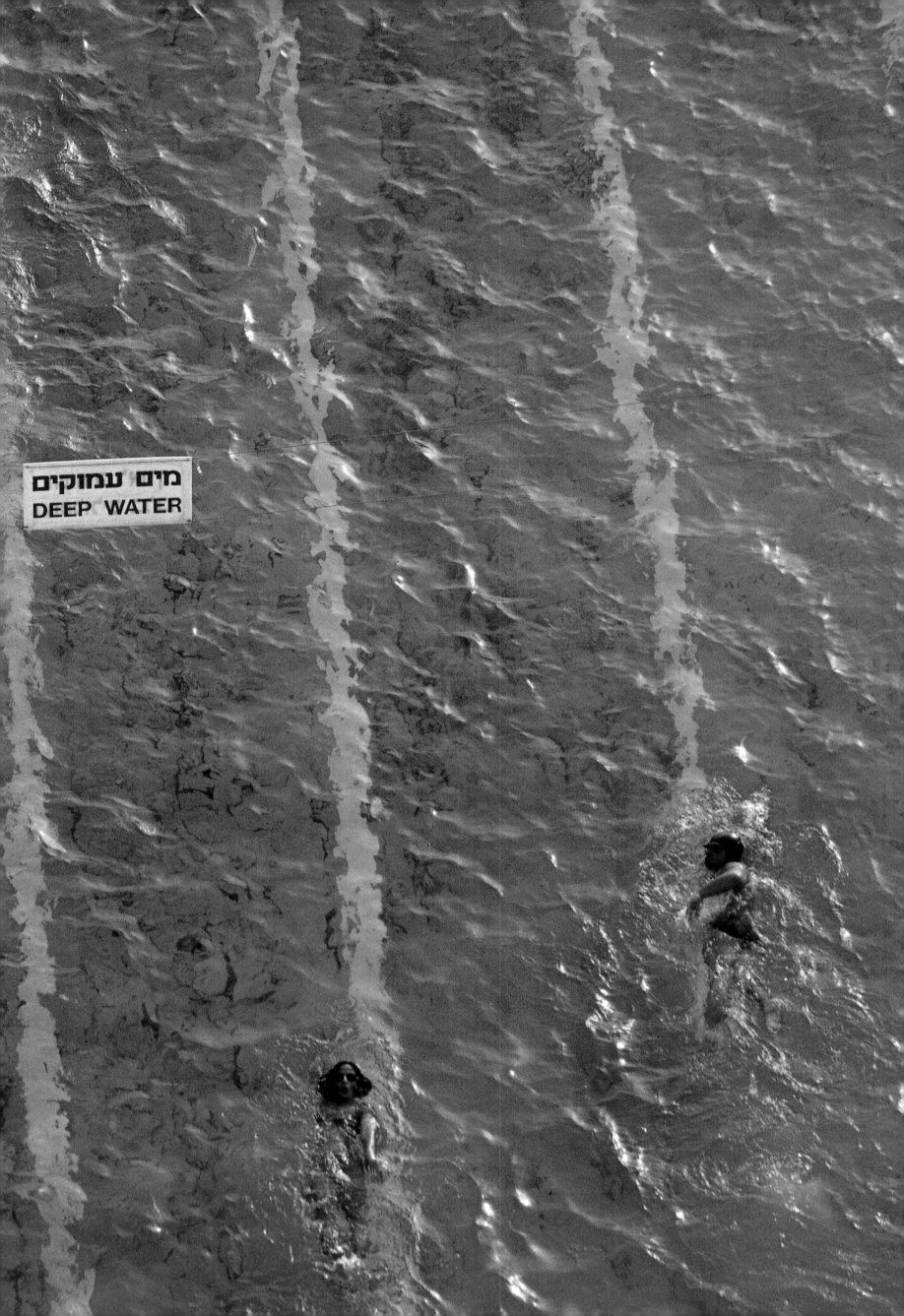

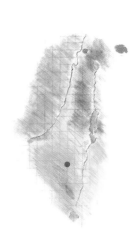

● **LEFT**

The switchbacked lanes of Independence Ascent climb steeply from the floor of Makhtesh Ramon crater in the central Negev Desert. The largest natural crater in the world—five miles (eight kilometers) wide and 1,000 feet (300 meters) deep—Makhtesh Ramon was formed not by a crashing meteor but by the forces of erosion. The Independence Ascent was built in 1954 as a safer route out of the crater than Scorpion Ascent, a road, close to the Jordanian border, that was subject to deadly terrorist attacks.

JAMES MARSHALL

● RIGHT

Desert flower farmer Dan Becker gives his three-year-old son, Arnon, a playful toss by the barren cliffs of the Arava Valley in the Negev Desert.

ACEY HARPER

● **ABOVE**

The fertile Jezreel Valley, Israel's breadbasket. Early Zionists bought most of Ha'emek (The Valley) from Arab landholders in the early 20th century. In a heroic effort, they drained the malarial swamps, and over the years, planted 125 million trees along the valley slopes. Though decidedly tranquil in this photograph, the Jezreel Valley is cited in the Bible's Book of Revelations as the site of Armageddon, the final battle between good and evil.

JOEL SARTORE

● ABOVE

New apartment buildings line King Solomon Street in Netanya, the Miami Beach of Israel. With its sandy Mediterranean beaches, affluent retirees and world-famous diamond industry, Netanya is one of Israel's largest and most prosperous seaside resorts.

RICK BROWNE

● **LEFT**

Israeli guards patrol a new border road being built between the Gaza checkpoints of Erez and Nahal Oz.

NIK WHEELER

● **ABOVE**

The banner reads "Shalom," the Hebrew word for peace. It was hung at the Erez checkpoint on the Gaza border by demonstrators from Israel's Peace Now movement.

NIK WHEELER

A Day in the Life of the Hai-Bar Nature Reserve

BY FRANS LANTING, ONE OF THE WORLD'S FOREMOST WILDLIFE PHOTOGRAPHERS

Part of the 8,000-acre Hai-Bar Arava Biblical Wildlife Reserve as viewed from above.

The Hebrew word for "wild life" is *hai-bar*, and in Israel, the center for native wildlife is the Hai-Bar Arava Biblical Wildlife Reserve. One of three hai-bar reserves (the others are in Haifa and under construction in the Golan), the Arava reserve was established on 8,000 acres of salt flats in the Negev near the Jordanian border.

Hai-Bar was created to reintroduce to Israel wild animal species mentioned in the Bible. The center also attempts to rescue native Israeli animals threatened with extinction.

Hai-Bar has had some notable successes. The white oryx, hunted nearly to worldwide extinction, disappeared entirely in Israel early in this century. Hai-Bar has reestablished herds of hundreds of white oryxes in the reserve and plans to reintroduce the animals into the wild. Other species were rescued in typical Israeli fashion. Mesopotamian fallow deer were smuggled out of Iran during the revolution there, and the Israeli Air Force air-lifted a flock of ostrich chicks out of Ethiopia.

World-renowned wildlife photographer Frans Lanting spent his Day in the Life of Israel observing Hai-Bar's desert denizens.

A big-eared fennec fox, smallest member of the fox family.

A southern wolf streaks across the desert.

Somali wild asses on the savanna at Hai-Bar. Wild asses disappeared in Israel during the Bronze Age (c. 3,500 BCE). These were brought to Hai-Bar from Iran.

● **LEFT**

The Mushroom, an arresting rock formation sculpted by erosion, is near King Solomon's Pillars in Timna Park, north of Eilat.
FRANS LANTING

● **ABOVE**

Scientist Reuven Epher uses sophisticated radio telemetry equipment to study the behavior of wolves in the Negev Desert.
FRANS LANTING

● LEFT

The saying goes, "In Tel Aviv, they dance; in Jerusalem, they pray; and in Haifa, they work." Since 1934, when the British completed modernization of the city's harbor, Haifa has been a major shipping, naval and industrial center. Despite its heavy industry, Haifa is also one of Israel's most beautiful cities. At a steel mill in Haifa's dock area, workers pour iron bars for Israel's brisk construction industry.

VERA LENTZ

● ABOVE

Sunset over the Paz facility in the Haifa Bay area.

JEFFERY ALLAN SALTER

● FOLLOWING PAGES

Camels caravan along the banks of the Dead Sea.

CLAUS MEYER

● ABOVE

The Mediterranean sun sets over the Tayelet, Tel Aviv's cafe-studded seaside promenade.

C. W. GRIFFIN

● RIGHT

In Jerusalem's East Talpiot neighborhood, Janice and Danny Azoulay sit down to a supper of cheese, salad and eggs with their three children, Dorie, Elad and Kelli. Danny Azoulay immigrated to Israel from Morocco; Janice lived most of her life in the United States. The Azoulays, both ceramic artists, are planning to move to Tzur Hadassah, a village of 200 families, to escape the daily stress of city life.

NICK KELSH

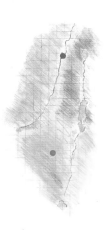

● **RIGHT**

At twilight, Yazaro Abata, an Ethiopian immigrant, returns with her nine-month-old son, Aviv, to their mobile home in a caravan site, a temporary housing settlement near Haifa. Since 1984, more than 21,000 Ethiopian Jews have been airlifted to Israel in dramatic rescue operations code-named Operation Moses and Operation Solomon. Ethiopia's Jews maintained Judaic customs for centuries in isolated villages on the Horn of Africa. Since their abrupt arrival in Israel during the 1984 and 1991 airlifts, thousands of Ethiopians—many of whom had never experienced modern conveniences such as plumbing and electricity—have been housed in absorption centers, transit camps and mobile homes. The Israeli government is now providing assistance to immigrants to move into new, permanent housing developments. Abata and her husband are hoping to move into a new home in Netanya within the next few months.

JEFFERY SALTER

● **FOLLOWING PAGES**

Sunset in the Negev Desert.

SHAI GINOTT

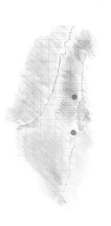

● **ABOVE**

Twilight at the Western Wall and the Temple Mount in Jerusalem.

PAUL CHESLEY

The lights of the Dead Sea Works, a processing plant that extracts minerals from the Dead Sea, blaze through the night in Sodom.

MOSHE SHAI

● ABOVE AND RIGHT

Musicians in the acclaimed Israel Philharmonic Orchestra tune up for the evening's performance in Tel Aviv. The orchestra, conducted by the renowned Zubin Mehta, boasts one of the largest subscribing symphony audiences in the world.

DOUGLAS KIRKLAND

● FOLLOWING PAGES

In Arava, more than 1,000 family members, friends and well-wishers attend an annual coming-of-age party for all of the community's 13-year-old boys and girls. Instead of holding more traditional Jewish *Bar* or *Bat Mitzvah* ceremonies, families on several of the area's moshavim join together for an evening of skits, videos and fireworks honoring all of the children who became teenagers during the year.

ACEY HARPER

● **LEFT**

Passionate fans of the Maccabi-Tel Aviv basketball team cheer their heroes during a tense playoff against local rival, Hapoel Tel Aviv sports club. The Maccabis were victorious (76-72) in front of 4,000 fans at the Yad Eliyahu arena.

Day in the Life photographer C. W. Griffin, who regularly covers the Atlanta Hawks of the NBA, watched both Israeli teams warm up before the game. Griffin said he knew almost immediately which team would prevail and set up his camera on the winning side of the arena for the most dramatic shots.

C. W. GRIFFIN

● **ABOVE**

Anxious sixth-grade kibbutzniks watch as their comrades wade across the Jordan River in the dark, holding onto a rope for safety. The chilly ordeal, near Kfar Blum kibbutz in the Upper Galilee, marks the youngsters' initiation into *Hashomer Hatzair* (The Youth Guard), run by the Mapam Socialist Party. Hashomer Hatzair is one of several youth organizations affiliated with Israel's political parties.

RAZI

● **ABOVE**

Night life in the New City:
Young Israelis unwind in a
Jerusalem discotheque.

PAUL CHESLEY

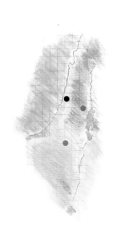

● **FOLLOWING PAGES**

● **ABOVE**

In his tent at Wadi Nafikh outside Beersheva, Sweilim Abublaya listens to an Arabic drama and drinks tea with his sons at the end of the day.

NINA BARNETT

Twenty-year-old singer/ songwriter Aviv Gefen poses on the floor of a Tel Aviv recording studio.

BARRY FRYDLENDER

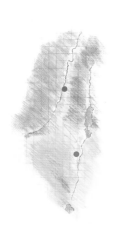

● **RIGHT**

Saxophonist Peter Wertheimer leads his band in 1960s jazz classics at the Omar Kayam night club in Jaffa.

ANTHONY BARBOZA

● **FOLLOWING PAGES**

A bellydancer whirls by evening guests at the Mamshit Camel Ranch, a Bedouin-style tourist center in Dimona, in the Negev Desert.

ANTHONY BARBOZA

EDITORS' NOTES

A Talmudic scholar in Jerusalem. **ALON REININGER**

A NOTE ON PLACE NAMES IN
A DAY IN THE LIFE OF ISRAEL

Place names in Israel are derived from two languages—
Hebrew and Arabic—that do not use the Roman alphabet,
and therefore, do not transliterate directly into English. Both
languages also have sounds which do not exist in English, just as
English has sounds, such as *ch* and *th*, which do not regularly
occur in Hebrew or Arabic.

To complicate matters further, English speakers over the
centuries have attached names to places, especially places of
Biblical significance, that differ from the names Israelis use for
the same places. For example, *Jerusalem* is called *Yerushalayim* in
Hebrew, *Sodom* is *S'dom* and what Christians refer to as the *Sea of*
Galilee is called *Yam Kinneret* in Hebrew.

Finally, the fractious politics of the region have spawned their
own divergent set of names and references. Israelis who favor
keeping certain territory occupied by Israel after the 1967 Six-
Day War refer to the area west of the Jordan River as Judea and
Samaria. Palestinians might refer to the same place as the Occupied Territories; others call it the Territories. We have opted for
the West Bank, as it seems to us to be the most geographically
based and therefore neutral term.

As a consequence of these divergent spellings and place names,
different maps and guidebooks use different sets of English
letters to represent the same place. In the English edition of *A*
Day in the Life of Israel, we have tried to avoid the political conno-

tations of place names to the extent possible and to choose the transliterations most familiar to most readers. Therefore, we use *Haifa*, not *Hefa: Tiberias*, not *Teverya;* and *Jericho*, not *Yeriho*. In some cases, it was a close call. For example, we refer to *Nazareth*, not *Nazerat*, because the Christian tradition in most English-speaking countries makes Nazareth most recognizable—even to Jews. On the other hand, we refer to Nazareth's neighbor city as *Nazerat Illit*, rather than Upper Nazareth, because no one calls this place Upper Nazareth. In cases like this, we also sometimes use two names, one in parentheses such as Safed (S'fat). We hope the pictures, which form the heart of this book, will be equally powerful and enjoyable in any language.

Plants and pants in Jerusalem. **RAGHU RAI**

A NOTE ON THE MAP USED IN A DAY IN THE LIFE OF ISRAEL

Throughout *A Day in the Life of Israel*, you are guided by a map in the upper left-hand or upper right-hand corner of the page. In each case, the map will show by means of a dot where the picture on the page was taken.

In this land of war and peace, something as simple as a map showing the borders of Israel is weighted with enormous political significance. For one thing, the borders of the country keep changing. On May 3, 1994, two days before *A Day in the Life of Israel* was photographed, Gaza, the strip of land south of Ashkelon, was administered by Israel. The Gaza Strip was shown on virtually all maps published in Israel as part of the country without any border line. On May 5, the day our photographs were made, Gaza had been turned over to the administration of the Palestinian Liberation Organization, and was probably no longer considered part of Israel by most people.

Maps of Israel in most English-language guidebooks delineate the area known variously as the West Bank, Judea and Samaria or the Occupied Territories with a dotted line. This line does not appear on maps published in Israel. As of this writing, there was talk of negotiations between Israel and Syria about returning parts of the Golan Heights. By the time this book is published, some of this territory might be returned to Syria—or it might not.

As we prepared to shoot *A Day in the Life of Israel*, we were interviewed by nearly every major magazine, newspaper and television network in Israel. The first questions were nearly always the same: Will you photograph in Gaza? In Jericho? On the West Bank? In the highly politicized atmosphere of Israel, these were loaded questions. The subtext was: For the purposes of this book, are these areas part of Israel or not? Will your book present a full picture of Israel or a censored one? Although we understand these are matters of great seriousness, we felt, in the end, they are not best answered by the editors of a coffee table book. We therefore encouraged the photographers to shoot freely throughout the area administered by Israel, and we use a map without borders—deftly avoiding these issues altogether. The reader, depending on his or her point of view, may draw the borders of Israel at will. — *The Editors*

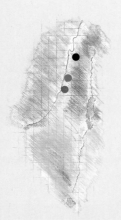

A Day in the Life of Israel Project Staff

● More than 60 world-renowned photographers, their assistants, friends and the *Day in the Life of Israel* project staff gathered on the roof of the Tel Aviv Hilton.
JAMES MARSHALL, ELDAD RAFAELI AND RAZI

EDITOR & PROJECT DIRECTOR
David Cohen

PRODUCER & PROJECT
CO-DIRECTOR
Lee Liberman

DIRECTOR OF PHOTOGRAPHY
Peter Howe

DESIGNER
Tom Morgan, Blue Design

ASSIGNMENT RESEARCH
Lee Liberman

PRODUCTION DIRECTOR
Ron Savir

WRITER
Susan Wels

FINANCE DIRECTOR
Devyani Kamdar

PRODUCTION COORDINATOR
Barry Sundermeier

LOGISTICS COORDINATOR
Linda Lamb

ASSIGNMENT COORDINATOR
Merav Peri

MASTER OF GUIDES AND
ASSISTANTS
Joshua Liberman

PRODUCTION ASSISTANTS
Cassy Liberman
Berry Liberman
Russell Sacks
Zoe Trigere-Besserman

PUBLICITY
United States: Molly Schaeffer
Israel: Patti Richards

PICTURE EDITORS
Howard Chapnick
Sandra Eisert,
The San Francisco Examiner
Bert Fox, *The Philadelphia Inquirer*
Laurie Kratochvil

COPY EDITOR
Amy Wheeler

RESEARCH CONSULTANTS
John Rothmann
Michael Jankelowitz
Alona Vardi

ATTORNEYS
Philip Feldman
Coblentz, Cahen, McCabe & Breyer

Joshua Rosensweig
Rosensweig, Shafran, Gera & Co.

LIASON
Peter Friend

PHOTOGRAPHERS' BIOGRAPHIES

NUBAR ALEXANIAN
American/Boston, Massachusetts
Alexanian is a documentary photographer whose work has been widely published in the *New York Times Magazine, Life, Fortune, GEO,* the *London Sunday Times* and others. His first book, *Stones in the Road: Photographs of Peru,* was recently published in the United States. His second book, *Where Music Comes From,* will be published in the fall of 1995. He has received numerous awards including a Fulbright Fellowship in 1983 for work in Peru. Alexanian found the best falafel he ever had across from the Fifth Station of the Cross in Jerusalem.

SHLOMO ARAD
Israeli/Tel Aviv
A professional photographer for 28 years who has concentrated on coverage of conflicts in the Middle East, Arad has been published widely in the Israeli press as well as in major European and American publications such as *The New York Times Magazine, Stern, VSD* and numerous others in Sweden and Great Britain. He was *Newsweek's* contract photographer in Israel for 15 years. In 1974, he was awarded the Anna Rivkin Bruck Prize and held a one-man exhibition in Tel Aviv. His photographs have appeared in many international exhibitions, and his photo album, *Bedouins: The Sinai Nomads* was published in Tel Aviv in 1984.

JANE EVELYN ATWOOD
American/Paris
Jane Evelyn Atwood was born in New York in 1947 and has been living in France since 1971. A member of Contact Press Images since 1988, she works primarily in the tradition of documentary photography, following individuals or groups of people (usually those on the fringes of society) for long periods of time. She is the author of three books—two about French prostitutes in Paris and one about the French Foreign Legion. She has won various international prizes and was the first recipient of the W. Eugene Smith Award in 1980 for her work on the blind. In 1987, she won a World Press Prize for "Jean-Louis—Living and Dying with AIDS." In 1990, she received the *Paris Match* Grand Prix du Photojournalisme, and in 1991 was granted the Canon Photo Essay Award for her work in women's prisons in the USSR. Her first retrospective, "Documents," was part of the Mois de la Photo in Paris in 1990-1991.

SHAHAR AZRAN
Israeli/New York
An Israeli photojournalist working in the United States since 1991, Azran has done assignments for the Israeli newspapers *Hadashot* and *Ma'ariv.* He is affiliated with Sygma Photo News Agency in New York City. His pictures have been published in *The New York Times, Fortune Magazine* and *The Washington Post,* among others.

● An elaborate lifeguard station in Herzlyia. **YUVAL HOSEN**

MICHA BAR'AM
Israeli/Ramat Gan
An active photographer since the 1950s, Bar'Am has been associated with Magnum Photos since 1967 when he teamed up with Cornell Capa to cover the Six-Day War. Bar'Am was a contract photographer for *The New York Times* from 1968 until 1992. He is a member of the International Center of Photography's International Advisory Council. He has been published and exhibited widely in Israel and abroad. Bar'Am's latest prize is the Israel Museum's Photography Prize for 1993. Bar'Am is the founding curator of the Photography Department at the Tel Aviv Museum of Art. He has a great beard.

ANTHONY BARBOZA
American/New York
Barboza began his photographic career in 1964 with the Kamoinge Workshop, under the direction of the revered African American photographer Roy DeCarava. His work has been published in *The New York Times Magazine, Life, Newsweek, Time, National Geographic, TV Guide, Elle, Vogue, US, McCall's, Vanity Fair, People, Details, Esquire, GQ, Harper's Bazaar, Self, Glamour, Woman's Day, Cosmopolitan, Playboy, Ms., Interview, The Village Voice, Ebony, Essence, Black Enterprise, Jet, Emerge* and *GEO.* At 50, Barboza still parties hard and is the father of many children.

NINA BARNETT
American/New York
Barnett is a freelance editorial photographer based in Manhattan, her hometown. Photography is a second career. Previously, Barnett edited photography books for eight years. After switching careers, her first major assignment was for *A Day in the Life of America* in 1986. Currently, Barnett does feature work for *The New York Times Magazine, Money, Fortune, Seventeen* and Whittle Communications, among others. Barnett got on this project by bribing the director with massive quantities of lox, white fish and bagels that she Federal Expressed from Zabar's in New York.

RICK BROWNE
American/Scotts Valley, California
Co-director of the forthcoming *A Day in the Life of Thailand,* Browne is a photojournalist specializing in travel photography and environmental portraiture for both editorial and corporate clients. He recently received

the silver medal from the Society of American Travel Writers. Browne was also director and co-editor of the photography book, *Hong Kong: Here Be Dragons,* and is under contract as photographic consultant to the world-renowned Monterey Bay Aquarium. Browne is known as the world's greatest optimist and a very good cook.

PAUL CHESLEY
American/Aspen, Colorado
Chesley is a freelance photographer who has worked with *National Geographic* since 1975, traveling regularly to Europe and Asia. He has completed more than 35 projects for the Society. Solo exhibitions of his work have appeared in museums in London, Tokyo and New York. *A Day in the Life of Israel* is the eleventh Day in the Life project for Chesley, a frequent contributor to *Life, Fortune, Time, Newsweek, Audubon, GEO* and *Stern.* Recent books including his work are *The Circle of Life, Mauritius, Hawaii, Colorado* and *America: Then & Now.* Paul shoots more film than any other *Day in the Life* photographer. We don't mind, though, since he also got the most pictures in the book.

● The Gordon Beach Club gardens.
PAUL CHESLEY

YOSSI COHEN
Israeli/Tel Aviv
Cohen is an up-and-coming young photographer in the Israel Defense Forces. He grew up in Tel Aviv and studied photography at Wizo High School for three years. Cohen joined the Photography Branch

of the Israel Defense Forces Spokesman's Unit in August 1992. Since then, he has seen a lot of action photographing the deportation of Hamas members from Israel in December 1992, Operation Accountability in July 1993 and the events following the Hebron Massacre in March 1994. Cohen says, "I intend to continue studying and working in the field of photography in the future." We think he will do well.

BARBARA D. DEMOULIN
American/Fort Worth, Texas
DeMoulin has been a fine portrait photographer for the last 10 years, owning her own studio for the last two. She has achieved the Masters level in the Professional Photographers of America. Her work has been published in several books, including *At the Rim,* a book on women's collegiate basketball. Although her work has been shown in numerous exhibitions, this is her first photojournalism assignment.

RAYMOND DEMOULIN
American/Forth Worth, Texas
An honorary photographer on this project, DeMoulin is known as "Saint Ray" to photographers everywhere for his support of photography during his 39 years at Eastman Kodak Company. If anyone is responsible for the continuing success of the *Day in the Life* series, it is Ray.

DAVID DOUBILET
American/New York
David Doubilet is one of the world's most accomplished underwater photographers. Born in 1946, he began snorkeling at the age of eight. By the age of 13, he was taking his first underwater photographs in the cold, green seas off the north New Jersey coast. After majoring in film and journalism at Boston University, he began his lifelong association with *National Geographic.* Since 1972, his work has been featured in more than 30 articles in the magazine, as well as in several of the Society's books.

● Israeli President Ezer Weizman greets Druze elders. **LEONARD FREED**

PHOTOGRAPHERS' BIOGRAPHIES

● River rafting on the Jordan River. **GILAD OPHIR**

Doubilet has received many awards for his work, including "Diver of the Year" from the Boston Sea Rovers, the prestigious Sara Prize from Italy's *Mondo Sommerso* magazine and honors from the National Press Photographers Association. His first book, *Light in the Sea*, was published in 1989. With his wife, Anne, also an experienced diver and photographer, he is the author of *Under the Sea from A to Z*, an underwater alphabet book for children published in 1991. The Doubilets live in New York City and Elberon, New Jersey, with their daughter, Emily, when not on assignment in some distant sea.

LEONARD FREED
American/New York

Leonard Freed began his professional career as a painter, but within a short time, he became a photojournalist. He has worked regularly for the *London Sunday Times*, *The New York Times Magazine*, *Stern* and *GEO*, traveling to all corners of the world. He covered the Middle Eastern wars and produced major essays on Poland, Asian immigration to England, North Sea oil development, violence in New York City and Spain since Franco, among many other diverse projects. Recent essays include "Vendetta in Crete," "Turkish Village," "Cyprus," "East Germany," "Gambling in Atlantic City," "Lebanon at War," "Death of Black Children in Atlanta, Georgia" and "The US Army in Germany." He has received grants from the New York State Council on the Arts and the National Endowment for the Arts.

Freed's photographs, first exhibited in 1960, have been included in numerous exhibitions including "The Concerned Photographer" series at The Riverside Museum in New York, the Smithsonian Institution in Washington, the National Museum in Jerusalem and the Matsuya in Tokyo. Books featuring Freed's photographs include *Deutsche Juden Heute* (1965); *Black in White America* (1968); *Seltsamespiele* (1970);

Made in Germany (1970); *Berlin*, part of Time-Life's *Great Cities of the World* series (1978); *Police Work* (1980); *La Danse Des Fidèles*, (1984) and *Leonard Freed*, an exhibition catalog by Galerie Municipal du Chateau d'Eau (1987).

BARRY FRYDLENDER
Israeli/Tel Aviv

In 1984, Frydlender received the Gerard Levy Prize from the Israel Museum in Jerusalem. One-man exhibitions of his work have been held at the Nikon Gallery in London, The Israel Museum in Jerusalem and the Photography Center of Athens. His work has been included in group shows in London, Jerusalem, New York, Tel Aviv, Helsinki and Berlin.

AVI GANOR
Israeli/Ramat Hasharon

Ganor was born in 1950 in Ramat Hasharon, Israel. He studied aeronautical engineering at the Technion in Haifa before traveling to the United States to study at the San Francisco Art Institute, the Pratt Institute and the Parsons School of Design in New York. Since 1977, Ganor has been working as a photographer and teaching at the Bezalel Academy of Art and Design in Jerusalem, Beit Zvi in Ramat Gan and Camera Obscura in Tel Aviv. Since 1991, he has been head of the department of computerized images at Camera Obscura.

CRISTINA GARCIA RODERO
Spanish/Madrid

Garcia Rodero specializes in fine-art photography. Her work has been published in several magazines, including *Lookout* and *El País*. Previously a drawing teacher, she now teaches photography at the Facultad de Bellas Artes de la Universidad Complutense de Madrid, where she first studied Spanish fiestas, customs and traditions. In 1985, she was awarded the Premio Planeta de Fotografía. Her book, *España Occulta*, is

widely admired by photographers around the world. Garcia Rodero is nearly impossible to reach, and we cannot believe she actually showed up for this assignment.

SHAI GINOTT
Israeli/Tel Aviv

Born in 1958 in Jerusalem, Shai Ginott is widely recognized as one of Israel's most talented "new photographers," with several published books to her credit. Ginott has served as Director of Photography at the Israel Nature Reserves Authority. Between 1985 and 1989, she was a guest lecturer at the Israel Professional Photographers' Association; Cambridge University; Hadassah College, Jerusalem; The University of Tel Aviv; The Hebrew University, Jerusalem, and The Ben-Gurion University of the Negev. In 1989 she was named "Best Nature Photographer" by *Israel Photographic Magazine*. Shai Ginott's clients include the Israel Defense Forces, *Land and Nature, Eretz*, El Al Airlines, Israel Ministry of Tourism, *Ma'ariv* (weekend supplement), the Jewish National Fund and *The Jerusalem Post*. A traveling exhibit of her photographs, "Nature and Landscape in Israel," commissioned by the Israel Foreign Ministry, is currently on display in several countries around the world.

YEHOSHUA GLOTMAN
Israeli/Maale Hagalil

Yehoshua Glotman was born in 1953 in Israel. He has studied photography in Jerusalem and at the Polytechnic of Central London in England. His involvement with photography encompasses both fine-art photography and documentary work. Glotman has taught at the Bezalel Academy of Art in Jerusalem for the past 11 years. He has exhibited his work in Israel and Europe and is the author of *An Israeli's Album* (1988). He is now living in a small village in the Upper Galilee with his wife and two children.

C. W. GRIFFIN
American/Miami

C. W. Griffin is a staff photographer for the *Miami Herald*. He also teaches advanced photojournalism at the University of Miami. His work has appeared in *Newsweek, National Geographic, Smithsonian* and the books *Songs of My People* and *The African Americans*. His work has been recognized by the National Press Photographers Association, which named him Military Photographer of the Year in 1980. He is the only African American ever to win this award.

LORI GRINKER
American/New York

Lori Grinker began her career in 1980, while still a student at Parsons School of Design, when an assignment about a young boxer was published as a cover story by *Inside Sports*. At that time, she met 14-year-old Mike Tyson, whom she has continued to photograph through the years. Her work has taken her to

the Middle East, Southeast Asia, Eastern Europe, the USSR, Africa and throughout the United States. She is particularly interested in the dramatic political and social changes now going on in Cambodia and Vietnam, where she has been traveling extensively since February 1989. Her photographs have been exhibited in museums and galleries in Paris, Amsterdam, Arles and New York and have been featured in *Life, The New York Times Magazine, Newsweek, People, The Sunday Times Magazine* (London), *Stern, GEO* and *Il Venerdì*.

Grinker has been a member of Contact Press Images since 1988. Her book, *The Invisible Thread: A Portrait of Jewish American Women* (1989), is an intimate collection of photographs exploring the diverse experience of Jewish women in the United States. A collection of images from the book toured the United States from 1990 to 1992. She is currently at work on two new book projects. One deals with indigenous peoples and their sacred relationship to the environment. The other, *When the War's Not Over*, studies the effects of war on veterans around the world.

CAROL GUZY
American/Washington, DC

Carol Guzy was born in Bethlehem, Pennsylvania on March 7, 1956. She lived there until 1978, when she completed her studies at Northampton County Area Community College, graduating with an Associate's degree in Registered Nursing. A change of heart led her to the Art Institute of Fort Lauderdale in Florida to study photography. She graduated in 1980 with an Associate in Applied Science degree in photography. While at the Art Institute, she interned at the *Miami Herald*. Upon graduation she was hired as a staff photographer. She spent eight years at the newspaper before moving to Washington, DC in 1988 and starting as a staff photographer with *The Washington Post*, where she is presently employed. Her assignments include both domestic and foreign stories. She is a member of the National Press Photographers Association and the White House News Photographers Association. She has been honored with numerous awards, including the prestigious Pulitzer Prize in Spot News photography. She was twice named Photographer of the Year by the National Press Photographers Association.

ACEY HARPER
American/Tiburon, California

Acey Harper is a freelance photographer based in Tiburon, California. He has traveled worldwide for such clients as *People, National Geographic* and *USA Today*. He is currently managing director of Reportage Stock. Harper lives in Tiburon, California with his wife and two daughters.

MICHAL HEIMAN
Israeli/Tel Aviv

Born in Tel Aviv in 1954, Michal Heiman studied photography at Hadassah College in

Jerusalem from 1977 to 1979. From 1982 to 1984, she studied painting and sculpting at the Art Teachers College in Ramat Hasharon. From 1984 to 1991 she worked as a freelance newspaper photographer, specializing in portrait photography. In 1992-93, Michal was curator of Camera Obscura Gallery in Tel Aviv and taught at the School of Film and Television in Jerusalem, Camera Obscura and the Hadassah Canadian WIZO College of Design in Haifa. She continues to curate the Camera Obscura Gallery and lecture in the School of Film and Television, Jerusalem and Camera Obscura, Tel Aviv. She has a very cute baby and a very nice husband.

ROBERT HOLMES
British / Mill Valley, California
Robert Holmes is one of the world's foremost travel photographers. He was the first person to receive the Society of American Travel Writers' Travel Photographer of the Year award twice, in 1990 and 1992. His work regularly appears in major travel publications, including *National Geographic, GEO, Travel & Leisure* and *Islands*. He has 15 books in print. His photographs have been exhibited widely and are included in both corporate and museum collections.

YUVAL HOSEN
Israeli / Ramat Hasharon
Hosen is currently working on a book about landscape design. He won first prize from the photography department of the Faculty of Architecture and Town Planning at the Technion in Haifa.

ED KASHI
American / San Francisco
Ed Kashi is a freelance photojournalist based in San Francisco whose work has appeared in *National Geographic, Time, Fortune, GEO, Life, Smithsonian, London Independent Magazine, Newsweek, Forbes* and *The New York Times Magazine*, among many other publications. He has dedicated the past three years to *National Geographic*, shooting cover stories on the Kurds, water problems in the Middle East and the Crimea.

The story on the Kurds, which Ed researched and proposed to the *Geographic*, took him to Iraq, Iran, Syria, Turkey, Lebanon and Germany for eight grueling months in refugee camps and bombed-out Kurdish villages. It will be published in book form by Pantheon in 1995.

Kashi won a 1991 National Endowment for the Arts grant for his documentary work on the Loyalist community in Northern Ireland. These photos represent three years of personal work and have been published in the United States, Britain, Spain, Sweden, Japan, Canada and Italy.

As a documentary photographer, Kashi spends much of the year on the road working on topics of concern to him. In past essays, he has dealt with the heroin problem in Poland, culture and nightlife in

Berlin, the return of the Soviet veterans from the Afghanistan war and life in Eastern Europe. His latest personal project took him to Cairo to explore the City of the Dead. The resulting essay will be published later this year in Audubon magazine and The *Observer Magazine* in London.

NICK KELSH
American / Philadelphia
A native of North Dakota, Kelsh has produced award-winning photos for *Time, Life, Newsweek, National Geographic, Forbes, Fortune,* and *Business Week*. In 1986, he left the *Philadelphia Inquirer* to co-found Kelsh Wilson Design, a company that specializes in design and photography for annual reports and other corporate publications. Kelsh pictures are featured on the covers of *A Day in the Life of China, America: Then & Now* and *The Jews in America*. Kelsh sends out great Christmas cards.

DOUGLAS KIRKLAND
Canadian / Los Angeles
Kirkland is one of the world's best-known glamour and personality photographers. His 30 years in the business include camera work

● Parasailing off the coast of Eilat. **SHAHAR AZRAN**

with Marilyn Monroe, Judy Garland, Barbra Streisand and Christie Brinkley. He was one of the founding members of Contact Press Images. Kirkland's books includes *Lightyears* (1989) and *ICONS* (1993). He has been married to the beautiful and vivacious Francoise Kirkland for more than 25 years.

ANTONIN KRATOCHVIL
Czechoslovakian / New York
Born in Czechoslovakia in 1947, Kratochvil has been working in the US as a freelance photographer since 1972. He continues to travel the world on assignment for *Discover Magazine, Newsweek, The New York Times, The Los Angeles Times, Smithsonian* and *Condé Nast Traveler*.

His work has appeared in numerous books, and he was named 1991 Photojournalist of the Year by the International Center of Photography. In 1992, he won a silver medal from the Art Directors Club of New York. Although Kratochvil is the most politically incorrect person alive, he has a wonderful spirit. No problem, man.

MIKI KRATSMAN
Israeli / Tel Aviv
Born in 1959 in Buenos Aires, Argentina, Miki Kratsman moved to Israel in 1971. From 1987 until the present, he has been a photographer for the daily newspaper *Hadashot* and the Spanish publications *Cambio 16* and *Diario 16*. From 1991 until 1992, Kratsman was a teacher at Ramat Gan School of Art. He founded and managed the photo lab at *Hadashot* and served as a medical photographer at the Sourasky Medical Center in Tel Aviv. Kratsman has been honored with several exhibits of his work. He contributes to *Newsweek, Time* and the French *Libération*.

HIROJI KUBOTA
Japanese / Tokyo
Born in 1939 in Tokyo, Kubota graduated with a Bachelor of Arts in Political Science from Waseda University, Tokyo, in 1962. He lived in New York and Chicago from 1962 until 1967 and became a freelance photographer in New York in 1965. Kubota has been a member of the renowned Magnum photo agency since 1971. His work has been published and exhibited worldwide and has been included in many books. His many awards include the prestigious Mainichi Art Award.

DANIEL LAINÉ
French / Paris
Lainé started his career as a freelance photographer for *Libération* and has worked

for *Partir* and *Grand Reportages*, completing numerous travel stories in South America and Africa. Lainé has been a correspondent in Western and Central Africa for Agence France Presse and a staff photographer for *Actuel*. Lainé's pictures have been featured in *A Day in the Life of America, A Day in the Life of Spain* and *The Circle of Life*. His own books include *Indios, Black Faces* and *Kings of Africa*.

FRANS LANTING
Dutch / Santa Cruz, California
Frans Lanting was born in Rotterdam, the Netherlands, in 1951. After obtaining a Master's degree in environmental economics in 1977, he came to the United States to study environmental planning. He decided to pursue a career in photography instead. In the past decade, he has been a professional nomad, documenting wildlife and man's relationship with nature around the world. Since 1985, Lanting has worked predominantly for *National Geographic*. His assignments have ranged from a search for the last white rhinoceros in Zaire, to a circumnavigation of remote South Georgia Island in the Antarctic by sailboat, to the first photographic coverage of the fabled pygmy chimpanzee in the jungles of the Congo Basin.

Lanting's work is featured regularly in leading magazines worldwide, including *GEO, Audubon, International Wildlife, Figaro* and *Stern*. His books include *Madagascar: A World out of Time*, published internationally in 1990. Photographs from his latest book, *Okavango: Africa's Last Eden*, appeared initially in *National Geographic* as the longest wildlife story ever published in the 100-year history of the magazine.

Lanting has received numerous awards, including top honors in 1988 and 1989 from World Press Photo for his work in Madagascar and the Antarctic. His Okavango story earned Lanting the title of Wildlife Photographer of the Year from the British Broadcasting Company in 1991.

VERA LENTZ
Peruvian / Lima
Vera Lentz was born in Peru and has lived in Europe and the United States. She freelances for major American and international publications. At present she is completing a book on Peru for W. W. Norton. She is associated with Black Star Photo Agency in New York.

ALEX LEVAC
Israeli / Jerusalem
Alex Levac was born in Tel Aviv in 1944. He graduated in psychology and philosophy from Tel Aviv University in 1967. In 1971, he graduated from London College of Printing, London, England with a degree in photography. Levac has been a freelance photographer in Brazil, London, Los Angeles and Israel. From 1983 until 1993, he was staff photographer for the daily newspaper *Hadashot*. In 1993, he won the Rita Poretzky award from the Tel Aviv Museum.

PHOTOGRAPHERS' BIOGRAPHIES

GERD LUDWIG
German / Los Angeles
A founding member of the Visum photo agency in Hamburg, Ludwig is a regular contributor to *GEO, Life, Stern, Fortune, Time* and *Newsweek*. He became a *National Geographic* contract photographer in 1992. Since then, he has worked on issue-driven subjects such as "The Broken Empire," a lengthy report about changes in the former Soviet Union. Ludwig is a veteran of numerous *Day in the Life* projects.

PASCAL MAITRE
French / Paris
Maitre has photographed conflicts the world over and has published his work in *GEO, Stern, Time, Life* and *Le Figaro*. He has published three books: *Rwanda* (1991), *Barcelona* (1989) and *Zaire* (1985). In 1986, Maitre won a World Press Photo award for his work in Iran. He is associated with the agency GLMR Associés/SAGA Images.

JAMES MARSHALL
American / New York
Co-founder of Pacific Rim Concepts, Marshall produced and edited *Hong Kong: Here Be Dragons*, published to critical praise in 1992. For the past 15 years he has traveled extensively in Europe and Asia, contributing work to international publications including *Newsweek, The New York Times, Smithsonian, Travel & Leisure* and *US News and World Report*. In 1987, he organized *Document: Brooklyn*, involving 45 photographers recording one week in the life of this mythic American community, and thus became hooked on big productions. He is co-director of *A Day in the Life of Thailand*.

SUSAN MEISELAS
American / New York
Susan Meiselas received her masters in education from Harvard University and her undergraduate degree from Sarah Lawrence College. While photographic advisor to the Community Resources Institute, she developed curricula using photography and animated film, and ran workshops for teachers and children in the South Bronx in New York. Supported by grants from the National Endowment for the Arts and the state arts commissions of South Carolina and Mississippi, she set up film and photography programs in rural southern schools.

Meiselas's first major photographic essay, spanning several years, focused on the lives of carnival strippers in New England. She joined Magnum Photos in 1976.

Meiselas' coverage of hostilities in Central America has been published worldwide by *The New York Times Magazine, The London Sunday Times, Time, GEO, Paris Match* and *Machete* among others. She won the Robert Capa Gold Medal from the Overseas Press Club in 1979 for her work in Nicaragua. Her two books are *Carnival Strippers* (1976) and *Nicaragua* (1981). Meiselas was an editor and contributor to the book *El Salvador: The Work of Thirty Photographers*

● In the Church of the Holy Sepulcher, Jerusalem.
CRISTINA GARCIA RODERO

and editor of *Chile from Within*.

Recently, Meiselas has been researching and photographing *In the Shadow of History: Kurdistan* for Random House. She has co-directed two films: *Living at Risk: The Story of a Nicaraguan Family* (1986) and *Pictures From a Revolution* (1991). Meiselas has also received the Leica Award for Excellence and the Photojournalist of the Year Award from the American Society of Magazine Photographers. In 1992, Meiselas was named a MacArthur Fellow. She received a Photographer's Fellowship from the National Endowment of the Arts in 1984 and was awarded an honorary degree in Fine Arts from Parsons School of Design in 1986.

CLAUS C. MEYER
German / Rio de Janeiro
The winner of many prizes and awards, Meyer was selected in 1985 by *Communications World* as one of the top annual-report photographers in the world. His excellence in color photography has been recognized by Kodak and Nikon, and in 1981 he won a Nikon International Grand Prize. He has published several books on Brazil, most recently a book on the Amazon in 1993.

GILAD OPHIR
Israeli / Tel Aviv
Ophir studied at the School of Visual Arts and Hunter College. His work has been exhibited in the United States in several solo and group exhibitions. Most notable are two solo exhibitions at the Bertha Urdang Gallery in New York and the Gray Art Galley at the University of East Carolina. Ophir has been exhibiting his work extensively since returning to Israel in 1988. He is currently preparing a one-person show at the Tel Aviv Museum, scheduled for autumn 1994. Ophir teaches photography and art at the Institute of Art in Oranim and at the Kalisher Art School in Tel Aviv. He is

a recipient of the William Graf Scholarship from Hunter College, the Israel American Foundation Scholarship and the Gerard Levy Prize for young photographers from the Israel Museum in 1992.

SYLVIA PLACHY
American / New York
Sylvia Plachy's photographs have appeared in many publications. Her own book, *Unguided Tour*, won the Infinity Award from the International Center of Photography in 1990. Her most recent exhibit, *The Call of the Street*, was shown at the Whitney Museum at Philip Morris in 1993. Her photographs are in the collection of the Museum of Modern Art and the Metropolitan Museum in New York. She is currently working on books about Eastern Europe and about "red light" districts in the United States.

LARRY PRICE
American / Fort Worth, Texas
A native Texan, Price began his photographic career at the *El Paso Times*. Later, he worked for the *Fort Worth Star-Telegram*, where he won a Pulitzer Prize for his coverage of the 1980 Liberian coup. His photographs from El Salvador and Angola for the *Philadelphia Inquirer* won him a second Pulitzer in 1985. His work has been honored by the Overseas Press Club, the National Press Photographers Association, the Associated Press and the World Press competition. Price is a seasoned contributor to the *Day in the Life* series.

ELDAD RAFAELI
Israeli / Tel Aviv
Rafaeli studied at the Camera Obscura School of Art and Tel Aviv University. He has photographed for *Tel Aviv* and *Seven Days* newspapers. His many exhibitions include shows at the Camera Obscura Gallery and the Tel Aviv Museum.

RAGHU RAI
Indian / New Delhi
Rai was born in December 1942. He qualified as civil engineer, but started taking photographs at the age of 24. Rai's photographs first appeared in the *Times of London* in the late 1960s. His major photo essays have appeared in various magazines and newspapers around the world, including *National Geographic, GEO, Life, Stern, Time* and *The New York Times*. Rai has been on the jury of the World Press Photo competition in Holland for two years. He has published eight marvelous books on different themes in India. A member of Magnum Photos since 1977, this is Rai's first *Day in the Life* assignment, but we hope not his last.

ALON REININGER
American / Israeli / Los Angeles
Following a stint as a commercial photographer and assistant cameraman in Israel, Reininger turned to photojournalism in 1973 during the October War, which he covered for UPI. Since then, he has traveled extensively, documenting political and social change throughout the world. His work has appeared in *Time, Life, The New York Times Magazine*, and *The London Sunday Times*. Reininger's coverage of the AIDS crisis has earned him awards from the National Press Photographers Association, the World Press Photo Foundation and the American Society of Magazine Photographers. He is a founding member of Contact Press Images.

RICK RICKMAN
American / Laguna Nigel, California
Rick Rickman has been working as a photographer for 17 years. During those years he has been assigned major stories all over the world. He contributes regularly to *Time* and *National Geographic* magazines. In 1985, he was presented the Pulitzer Prize for Spot News Photography. Some of his favorite assignments have been with past *Day in the Life* projects. He is a very happy guy who laughs a lot.

RAZI (RICHARD ROBINOWITZ)
Israeli / American / Tel Aviv
Born in New York, Razi immigrated to Israel in 1987, where he has spent the past seven years photographing for the weekend magazine sections of *Yediot Aharonoth*, Israel's largest-circulation daily. His work has also appeared in *The Jerusalem Post*. His own projects have taken him to Egypt, Turkey, Poland and Brazil.

STEVE RUBIN
American / Baltimore, Maryland
Rubin's work is influenced by the documentary tradition of the 1930s and by his academic training in sociology. Undergraduate fieldwork among Gypsies led him to documentary photography, where he felt the concerns of sociology could be communicated visually. He has photographed the plight of Kurdish refugees, the destruction of the Ecuadorian rain forest, political turmoil

in Pakistan and the transition to democracy in Chile. Closer to home, he has covered stories that include illegal immigration, the health care crisis and the not-so-romantic life of hoboes. He is currently an Alicia Patterson Foundation Fellow, completing a long-term photo essay, "Poverty in Vacationland: Life in a Backwoods Maine Community." He has been honored with the Leica Medal of Excellence, a New York Foundation for the Arts Photography Fellowship, and an Award of Excellence from the National Press Photographers competition. He was a finalist for the W. Eugene Smith Award in Humanistic Photography in 1992 and 1993. His work has been published in *The New York Times Magazine, The Independent Magazine, Stern, GEO, L'Express, Time, Newsweek, The Village Voice* and *Outtakes* among others. He is represented by JB Pictures, New York.

DAVID RUBINGER
Israeli/Jerusalem
David Rubinger, perhaps Israel's most respected photographer, was born in Vienna in 1924 and came to Israel—then Palestine—in 1939 with Youth Aliyah. He spent the first years on a kibbutz and, at the age of 18, joined the British Army during World War II. It was in service with the Jewish Brigade in Europe that he became interested in taking pictures. Returning to civilian life, he settled his family in Jerusalem and determined to turn what was a hobby into his life's work. Freelancing for several years, he was invited in 1951 to join *Ha'Olam-Hazeh* magazine, covering the Kastner-Grunwald trial. Since then, he has covered nearly every history-making event in the Middle East for *Time* and *Life*.

RUSSELL SACKS
South African/Tel Aviv
Sacks is a talented young photographer who is traveling the world making pictures. He worked in the *Day in the Life of Israel* office as an assistant, asked for a place on the team, and made the best of it, getting two pictures in the book. We hope to see more from him.

HANA SAHAR
Israeli/Ramat Gan
Hana Sahar currently works as a magazine photographer in Israel. She has been represented in several exhibitions in Israel and received a scholarship from the French government.

JEFFERY ALLAN SALTER
American/Miami
In high school, all his classmates called him "the cameraman." Now they know him as Jeffery Allan Salter, the award-winning photojournalist who has covered such global events as the bombing of the Pan Am airliner over Lockerbie, Scotland, and the deadly Haitian elections of November 1987. Currently, Salter is a staff photographer with *The Miami Herald.* Previously, he worked for *Newsday, The Bergen Record, The Virginian Pilot/*

Ledger Star and *Navy Times.* Among his many awards: Leica Medal of Excellence Finalist, Atlanta Seminar on Photojournalism, Photographer of the Year, New Jersey Photographer of the Year, American Photographer's New Face in Photojournalism Finalist, numerous first-place awards from the New York Press Photographers Association and an Excellence in Photojournalism award from Sigma Delta Chi. His work has been included in recent books such as *The African Americans* and *Songs of My People.*

EMMANUEL SANTOS
Australian/Melbourne
A Filipino immigrant in Australia since 1982, Santos has produced photo essays and exhibitions on the human experience in China, Japan, India, the Philippines, Poland and Australia. His work has appeared in both Australian and worldwide publications. He has been working for a decade on a project on the lost tribes of Israel. He is a contributing photographer for Gamma Presse Images in Paris and a founding director of the M-33 Photo Agency in Melbourne.

● A dance recital in Tel Aviv.
HANA SAHAR

JOEL SARTORE
American/Lincoln, Nebraska
Sartore began his photography career as a photo intern with *The Wichita Eagle* in 1984, becoming its Director of Photography in 1990. He has been a contract photographer with *National Geographic* magazine since 1992. Among his honors are the Award of Excellence, Magazine Photographer of the Year category in the 1992 Pictures of the Year competition and 1986 Photographer of the Year, National Press Photographer's Association, Region 7.

MOSHE SHAI
Israeli/Ramat Gan
A photojournalist since 1980, Moshe Shai has worked for the *Hadashot* daily newspaper

for ten years and lately has joined the photography staff of *Ma'ariv* daily newspaper. His works appear in various Israeli photography books. Shai has taken part in group exhibitions in galleries and museums in Israel and abroad. He works as a local correspondent for major foreign newspapers and news services.

DUBY TAL
Israeli/Tel Aviv
Originally a landscape photographer, Duby Tal has been working for the past few years on aerial photography. As a former Israeli Air Force pilot, he unifies his two passions, flying and photography. His main attention is on light and its specific appearance in Israel, but his interest extends to color perception, design composition, abstract forms and graphic and structural perspectives. Tal has published three books, the best-selling *Skyline* (1990), *Jerusalem-Skyline* (1993) and *Archaeology-Skyline* (1994). His photographs have also appeared in magazines, books and exhibitions in Israel and abroad.

SHABTAI TAL
Israeli/Tel Aviv
Born in Israel in 1939, Tal graduated from Bezalel Academy of Art in Jerusalem. He has been a press photographer since 1961. Highlights of his coverage include the Six-Day War in 1967 for *Time* and *Life*, the Yom Kippur War and the Israel-Egypt peace process (in Israel, Egypt and Washington), the Intifada, the war in Lebanon (1982) and the Gulf War for *Stern*. Until 1991, Tal was bureau chief for *Stern* magazine in Israel. Today, Tal is a freelance photographer and correspondent for various German magazines. His exhibition "Man at War" was shown at the Jewish Museum in New York in 1974. His most famous photograph is a portrait of Israel's first prime minister, David Ben Gurion, that was printed in a widely circulated poster format and eventually became the most well-known portrait photo of Ben Gurion.

SCOTT THODE
American/New York
Scott Thode is a dedicated photographer whose work has appeared in *Life, Newsweek, The Independent, GEO, Il Venerdì* and many other North American and European publications. His work has been exhibited at the Visa Pour L'Image photo festival in Perpignan, France, in the Electric Blanket AIDS Project and at the P.S. 122 Gallery in New York City. In 1992, Thode was a finalist for the W. Eugene Smith Memorial Grant in Humanistic Photography. He won a first place at the Pictures of the Year competition sponsored by the National Press Photographers Association and took second place at the Gordon Parks Commemorative Photography Competition. Scott lives in New York City with his wife, Kathy Ryan, and their dog, Buster.

NIK WHEELER
British/Los Angeles
Nik Wheeler was born in Hitchin, England. He studied French and drama at Bristol University and French Civilization at the Sorbonne, Paris. Wheeler's world travels began in Athens, where he taught English. His photographic career began in Bangkok, where he co-published a guide book to Thailand. In 1967, Wheeler moved to Vietnam as a combat photographer and joined United Press International during the 1968 Tet Offensive. In 1970, he went to the Middle East and covered the Jordanian Civil War for *Time*, the October War for *Newsweek* and did assignments for *National Geographic* and *Paris Match*. In 1974, he moved to Paris and covered such diverse international events as the fall of Saigon, the Montreal Olympics, the US presidential elections and the coronation of the King of Nepal. Since 1977, he has been living in Los Angeles doing assignments for *National Geographic, GEO, International Wildlife* and travel magazines such as *Travel and Leisure, Travel Holiday, Islands* and *Departures*.

Wheeler's books include *Return to the Marshes* (1977), *Iraq—Land of Two Rivers* (1980), *This Is China* (1981) and *Cloud Dwellers of the Himalayas* (1982). Since 1986, he has been co-publisher and principal photographer for the *Insider's Guides*. In addition to photography, he has written articles and columns for *Travel and Leisure, Islands* and *Aramco World*. In 1988, he was named Photographer of the Year by the Society of American Travel Writers.

MARINA YURCHENKO
Russian/Moscow
After two years on the geography faculty of Moscow State University, Yurchenko decided to pursue a career in photojournalism. She has worked for *Sputnik* and the weekly *Moskovskiye Novosti* (*Moscow News*), and has been a correspondent for the Novosti Press Agency since 1981. Yurchenko counts among her photographic specialties art, theater, religion and daily life.

MEMO ZACK
Israeli/New York
Zack was born in Israel and lived there until he completed his military service. In 1962, Zack moved to New York City. After a 16-year career in the performing arts as a dancer and after completing a three-year program at City College of New York's Film Institute, he changed direction. With the encouragement and support of the renowned fashion photographer, Neal Barr, Zack decided to become a photographer. He spent five years as Barr's assistant and studio manager. In 1970, he left and opened his own studio specializing in fashion and beauty photography. During the past two years, Zack has spent half the year in New York City shooting for fashion and beauty clients and the other half traveling the world.

A Day in the Life of Israel Scrapbook

BRIEF ENCOUNTER
Photographers, staff and assistants are briefed at the Tel Aviv Hilton.
BARRY SUNDERMEIER

DYNAMIC DUO
Project Directors Lee Liberman and David Cohen.
MICHAL HEIMAN

I WENT DOWN TO NAZARETH
Photographer Joel Sartore and his assistant, Yoav Elkobi, in front of the Church of the Annunciation.
JOEL SARTORE

THEN YOU HEAD UP THE JORDAN RIVER AND TURN RIGHT AT THE SEA OF GALILEE
Production Director Ron Savir tells photographer Carol Guzy of *The Washington Post* where to go.
RICK BROWNE

DANCES WITH LAMBS
Logistics Coordinator Linda Lamb does her famous "Shalom, Shalom dance" **BARRY SUNDERMEIER**

AMERICAN KNOW HOWE
Day in the Life of Israel Photography Director, former Gap model and new American Peter Howe.
BARRY SUNDERMEIER

BADGES ... WE DON'T NEED NO STINKIN' BADGES
Photographers' credentials laid out in the *Day in the Life of Israel* office. **BARRY SUNDERMEIER**

KODAK GOLD
Kodak's Colin Wade and Steve Hunt and Delta Film's Sammy Knaffo deliver 4,000 rolls of film to Project Director David Cohen, assisted by Kara and Willie Cohen.
BARRY SUNDERMEIER

HERTZ SO GOOD
All 60 *Day in the Life* photographers prepare to start their engines at the Hertz/Kesher rental car lot near Ben Gurion Airport. **JAMES MARSHALL**

CAMERA SHAI
Israeli photographer Moshe Shai gets a leg up in the Dead Sea.
MOSHE SHAI

A Day in the Life of Israel Scrapbook

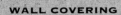

WALL COVERING
Photographer Bob Holmes sports a paper *yarmulke* at Jerusalem's Western Wall. **RICK BROWNE**

IT'S A BIRD ... IT'S A PLANE. .. NO, IT'S SIX WORLD-CLASS PHOTOGRAPHERS BURNING FILM
James Marshall, Robert Holmes, Acey Harper, Claus Meyer, Rick Browne and Nik Wheeler on the Haas Promenade in Jerusalem. **ANTHONY BARBOZA**

BOUNCING CZECH
Photographer Antonin Kratochvil holds forth in an Old City market stall. Kratochvil won the *Day in the Life of Israel* best answer award. When asked by El Al security why he went to Beersheva, he replied, "Why the *#@# not, man?" **SYLVIA PLACHY**

BOTTOM OF THE WORLD, MA
Project director David Cohen, Willie Cohen, five, Production Coordinator Barry Sundermeier, Logistics Coordinator Linda Lamb, Lucas Cohen (three months) and Finance Director Devyani Kamdar at the lowest point on earth. **NACHUM YARDENI**

ROMAN AROUND
Day in the Life writer Susan Wels at the Cardo Culinaria restaurant in Jerusalem. **LINDA LAMB**

MEET THE PRESS
Project Director David Cohen is interviewed by Osrat Levy of Israel's Channel 2, while Lee Liberman deals with Channel 1. **RON SAVIR**

TOWER OF POWER
Photographers Acey Harper, Vera Lentz, Jeffrey Allan Salter, Carol Guzy, C. W. Griffin and Emmanuel Santos at the farewell party at Jerusalem's Tower of David in the Old City. **ANTHONY BARBOZA**

ROLL OVER, LEONARDO
Photographers and staff reenact The Last Supper in the Cardo Culinaria in Jerusalem. **A NICE MORMON FELLOW FROM CALIFORNIA WHO WAS SLIGHTLY SHOCKED**

LOBBYING EFFORT
Photographers and staff gather for drinks in the lobby of the Holiday Inn, Crown Plaza. **SYLVIA PLACHY**

THE EYES HAVE IT
Picture Editors Bert Fox, Laurie Kratochvil, Peter Howe, Howard Chapnick and Sandra Eisert. **BARRY SUNDERMEIER**

ON A ROLL
Logistics Coordinator Linda Lamb collects film from Yuval Hosen and Daniel Lainé. **BARRY SUNDERMEIER**

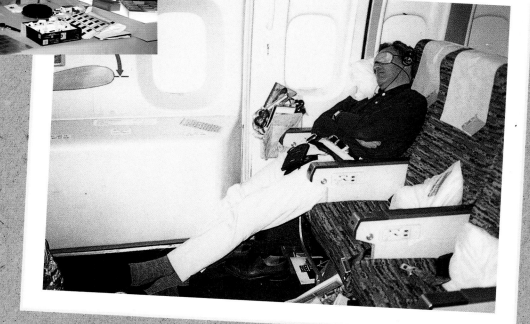

VISIONS OF KODACHROME DANCED IN HIS HEAD
On the way home from Israel, Photography Director Peter Howe catches a nap at 30,000 feet. **ANTHONY BARBOZA**

THE ASSOCIATION FOR PROMOTING TOURISM IN ISRAEL

The Association for Promoting Tourism in Israel is a nonprofit organization that assists the Ministry of Tourism through independent fundraising from private sources.

The association produces informational material, organizes seminars, supports marketing projects and generally serves as a driving force in tourism development. One of the best examples of its activities is its sponsorship of *A Day in the Life of Israel*.

ISRAEL MINISTRY OF TOURISM

Israel's Ministry of Tourism facilitates tourism in a variety of ways, including infrastructure planning, training professionals for every branch of the industry, providing verbal, printed and electronic information and producing films, slides and multimedia shows. Its offices abroad arrange seminars for travel agents and workshops for tour operators. They also work closely with airlines, the tourism press and the general media. The Ministry hosts travel journalists, TV crews and travel agents, and participates in dozens of tourism fairs each year throughout the world.

The Ministry of Tourism is also active in promoting investments, turning archaeological excavations into tourist sites, assisting ecology rescue operations, developing parks and promenades, restoring historical and religious sites, and helping to create employment in tourism enterprises.

The Ministry of Tourism markets Israel as an ancient yet modern tourist destination through the Israel Government Tourist Offices stationed overseas.

EL AL ISRAEL AIRLINES LTD.

El Al, Israel's national carrier, is the link between Israel and four continents, serving more than 40 cities in Europe, North America, Africa and Asia. El Al, with its heart in Israel, is the number one promoter of tourism to Israel. With 74 locations worldwide, El Al's professional staff is qualified to offer the traveler advice and assistance on a wide range of tourism topics in the land of Israel. As the airline that knows Israel

best, El Al is indeed proud to be among the sponsors of *A Day in the Life of Israel*, which artistically portrays scenes of everyday life in our country.

MORIAH HOTELS, LTD.

Israel's Moriah Hotel Chain includes six hotels offering a total of more than 1,700 rooms. There are Moriah Hotels in all of Israel's leading resorts and tourist centers: Jerusalem, Tiberias (the Sea of Galilee), the Dead Sea (two hotels), Eilat and Tel Aviv, making the Moriah Hotel chain second to none and the perfect choice for holidays in Israel.

Each hotel boasts a superb location and offers a full range of superior facilities for individuals, groups and conferences. The Moriah Hotel chain is affiliated with SRS and has earned an excellent reputation throughout the travel industry worldwide.

THE EASTMAN KODAK COMPANY

Eastman Kodak Company, the world leader in photography, produces films, papers and chemicals for professional and amateur use; electronic imaging products; motion picture films; copier-duplicators; and hundreds of other products for business and industry, health care and the home. The company employs more than 110,000 people worldwide, 57,000 of them in the U.S. In 1993, Kodak revenues totaled more than $16.4 billion, with nearly half coming from sales outside the U.S.

PAZ OIL COMPANY LTD.

Paz Oil Company, the leading petroleum company in Israel, supplies about 40 percent of local petroleum products. Together with some 20 subsidiaries, affiliates and a nationwide marketing network, Paz is a highly integrated concern involved in every aspect of the country's petroleum industry, including purchase of crude oil, production of fuels and lubricants, marine and land transportation, bulk storage of refined products and an extensive nationwide network of service stations identified by the distinctive yellow and black triangle.

The three largest Paz subsidiaries manufacture and market lubricants and solvents (Paz Lubricants and Chemicals Ltd.), bituminous products, glues and

heat-retardant products (Pazkar Ltd.) and Liquefied Petroleum Gas (Pazgas Ltd.).

BANK HAPOALIM

Bank Hapoalim is proud to be a part of *A Day in the Life of Israel*. As Israel's leading bank, Bank Hapoalim is an important contributor to the economy of this rapidly growing nation. Serving both the business community and the individual customer, Bank Hapoalim offers the full range of sophisticated, diversified services required by a modern society. Both domestically and abroad, every day Bank Hapoalim serves its customers through 350 branches, subsidiaries and representative offices in 17 countries.

Bank Hapoalim's participation in Israel's daily life has a long history, dating back to the 1920s. Since then, it has played a major role in the growth of Israel's industry, agriculture, infrastructure and trade. Today the Bank Hapoalim Group in Israel is comprised of six commercial banking institutions and numerous companies engaged in a variety of businesses, including investment banking, credit cards, provident and mutual fund management, leasing and insurance. These financial interests are complemented by involvement in high-tech industries, tourism and recreation facilities, energy, real estate and other economic sectors. Overseas, the bank focuses on wholesale banking and private banking services, which cater to select clients seeking personal service and global facilities.

DELEK THE ISRAEL FUEL CORPORATION LTD.

Delek is one of Israel's major importers of crude oil and a leading distributor of petroleum products.

Delek operates a network of 175 service stations throughout the country. It also carries out oil and gas exploration off the Tel Aviv shoreline.

Delek has investments in the petrochemical, chemical, storage and packaging industries. It is involved in retail trade through its holding in one of Israel's largest supermarket chains. Delek holds the Mazda automobile franchise for Israel and has investments in an emergency towing and roadside repair company.

Delek has a long history of community involvement. Through the Delek Fund for Science, Education and Culture, students engaged in research and development and technical training are granted scholarships for further study. The Fund also supports the Perach Tutorial Project, which pairs mentors with disadvantaged students to encourage educational excellence and positive social change.

It is with great pride that Delek sponsors the publication of this special volume, a visual celebration of the many facets of Israel.

ISRAEL DISCOUNT BANK

Israel Discount Bank was founded in 1935 by Leon Recanati, and has since developed into one of the country's largest three banks, with assets totaling $17.2 billion. The bank offers a broad range of local and international services, and its domestic subsidiaries include the Discount Mortgage Bank, Mercantile Discount Bank and the Discount Bank for Industrial Finance. In addition, the bank has substantial investment in the First International Bank of Israel.

Overseas subsidiaries include Israel Discount Bank of New York, the largest Israeli-owned bank in the USA, Israel Discount Bank of Canada and Discount Bank (Latin America).

CLAL (ISRAEL) LTD.

A leading business group, Clal (Israel) Ltd. was established in 1962. During the 1960s and 1970s, Clal expanded through a series of mergers and acquisitions to become one of Israel's leading investment companies.

The company oversees more than 150 operating companies located both in Israel and abroad. Clal's activities are focused in five main areas: industry, trade, construction and real estate, insurance and capital markets. Clal has also developed substantial expertise in the management of investments, creating conditions conducive to the development of companies within the group, whose operating policies emphasize management independence and initiative. These companies also enjoy professional management and consultancy services under the Clal umbrella.

Clal's portfolio of assets and its

operating policy have created an ideal basis for continued growth, enabling the group to take advantage of business opportunities and develop promising markets. The group's achievements are also founded upon strong capital backing and excellent liquidity, resulting in a broad base to raise capital on the Tel Aviv Stock Exchange and stock exchanges abroad. Securities of 30 Clal companies are traded on the Tel Aviv Stock Exchange, and some are considered Blue Chip stocks playing a major role in trading activities. Securities of six companies are publicly traded in the United States and on other foreign stock exchanges.

Clal's future direction has been shaped by evaluating and developing the strengths and keeping abreast of changes in the international and domestic business environment. The unification of the Common Market countries, the principal market for Israeli products, and other developments have enabled Clal to develop new trade channels, including new markets in Eastern Europe. The Clal group is also likely to benefit from trading experience in Latin America, as well as economic opportunities in Japan, China and Southeast Asia in the wake of strengthened trade ties between Israel and these regions.

In Israel, there has been a renewed emphasis on economic growth to enable the absorption of new immigrants and to fully realize their potential, ensuring the rapid development of vital local markets and favorable conditions for increasing exports. Concurrently, the peace process with Palestinians and neighboring Arab countries is bound to lead to regional prosperity and provide access to nearby markets. These conditions make Clal a potential strategic partner for any investor planning business investment in Israel.

THE ASSOCIATION OF ISRAELI INSURANCE COMPANIES

In 1957, with the introduction of shared underwriting, Israel's major insurance companies decided to establish an umbrella organization to represent them on common issues. Ten years later, the companies decided to pursue their joint interests through the founding of a limited company. The

Association of Life Insurance Companies of Israel, Ltd. consists of all 22 Israeli companies selling life insurance. The association's management is elected by shareholders and represents the companies in their dealings with the government and the public. The chairman of the board of directors is Mr. A. Levy. The managing director is Mr. S. Golomb.

THE ISRAEL INSURANCE ASSOCIATION

The Israel Insurance Association was established in 1949 as the official representative organization for insurance companies in Israel. Its purpose is to deal with important common issues concerning the insurance business, particularly its relations with the government as well as other authorities and similar foreign institutions. The association now encompasses 31 insurance companies—Israeli and foreign—in all areas of insurance except life insurance.

The association operates a pool for compulsory high-risk motor-vehicle insurance and provides automobile insurance for tourists. It operates the Insurance Institute and the Insurance Companies Clearance Centre, Ltd. The chairman of the association is Mr. R. Ben Shaul. The managing director is Mr. S. Golomb.

ISCAR

Established in 1952 and privately owned, Iscar is a multinational company producing and marketing carbide and ceramic cutting tools for the metal removal industry. The focus is on innovation, quality products and service. Exports, which account for 97 percent of Iscar's total turnover, are marketed via a worldwide network of more than 40 subsidiaries and agents.

In addition to long-established relationships in the United States, Canada, Europe and the Far East (including Japan), Iscar has recently initiated activities in Mexico, South America, Eastern Europe, Russia, India and China.

Iscar revolutionized turning-tool technology in the late 1970s with its Self-Grip tool system for parting and cutting off. During the next decade its

Grip tool spin-offs were introduced: Cut-Grip, Top-Grip and Heli-Grip (Heliface and Do-Grip). Iscar entered the 1990s with a unique approach to milling technology as represented by the Helimill, Helistar and Heliquad systems.

Iscar is interested in exploring possibilities for cooperative activities in marketing and distribution, joint ventures and the exchange of know-how. Iscar employs a total of 1,200 people; estimated revenues for 1994 are more than $200 million.

THE FEDERATION OF ISRAELI CHAMBERS OF COMMERCE (FICC)

FICC—The Federation of Israeli Chambers of Commerce—is one of Israel's major business organizations. With its finger on the pulse of the country's economy, the federation is regarded as one of the most influential and dynamic organizations in Israel. Strictly nonprofit, nonpolitical and nonpartisan, FICC is dedicated to a market economy and free enterprise. As the country's largest association of employers, FICC is one of the leading members of the coordinating council of Israel's economic organizations, and represents the interests of Israel's business sector, including export and import, wholesale and retail services, banking, computers, advertising, financial services and most other economic activities. FICC has been at the forefront of globalizing Israel's foreign trade, as well as fostering economic relations with its neighbors

within the framework of the Middle East peace process.

THE TEL AVIV HILTON

The Tel Aviv Hilton is a luxury five-star deluxe property with 595 rooms and suites, making it Israel's largest and some say its finest hotel. Located in the heart of the city on the Mediterranean seashore overlooking a marina and surrounded by beautiful Independence Park, the Tel Aviv Hilton provides the superb setting for a happy, fulfilling vacation or rewarding business trip. The hotel was proud to serve as the headquarters for *A Day in the Life of Israel.*

HERTZ/KESHER RENT-A-CAR

"Going the Extra Mile"
Hertz started operating in Israel in 1965 and today has 15 locations and a fleet of 1,800 vehicles including leasing operations.

Hertz's slogan of "Commitment to Excellence" permeates its operation— the high quality of its staff, aesthetic rental locations and a top-class rental fleet ranging from luxury vehicles to economy cars at competitive rates. All of these factors combine to give Hertz customers the best service possible.

Hertz Business Class Club provides frequent customers with benefits including discounts, upgrades and preferential reservations.

The Hertz International No. 1 Club makes available to customers a free International Hertz Credit Card that is very useful when reserving a Hertz vehicle anywhere in the world.

Air control tower activity at Hazor AFB. **SHABTAI TAL**

FRIENDS AND ADVISORS

● Sheik Saed Mansour in the village of Isfiya. **PASCAL MAITRE**

Sharon Abbady
Michael Abeles
Isaac Abraham
Joe Abrams
Sweilim Abublaya & Family
Debbie Adelsky
Ruth Adler
Herb Alexander
Rick Allen
Ziva Almagor
Anne Amdur
Amir Arad
Joan Armstrong
The Ascherman Family
Natalie Asseo
Irit Atzmon
Dr. Clinton Bailey
Monica Baltz
Jenny Barry
Suzy Barry
The Bechelli's Gang
Dan & Naomi Becker
Michael Ben-Abu
Mordechai Ben Ari
Shashana Ben Benishta
Tali Benbenisty
Danny Ben-Ezra
Sylvi Ben Hakon
Janie Joseland Bennett
R. Ben Shaul
Michal Ben Tovim
Bippin and Bharti Bhayani
Carole Bidnick
Zadik Bino
Zev Birger
Susan Bloom
Miri Bode
Kathryn Boschetto
Muriel Bouaziz

Ayellet Brand
Barbara and Stuart Brenner
Arnon Brookstein
Carl Broussard
The Browdie Family
Rodd Buckle
John Bull
Benjamin Cahlon
Robert Cambra
Woodfin Camp
Arthur Caplan
Clayton Carlson
David Carriere
Robert Cave-Rogers
Mike Cerre
Ani Chamichian
Jeanette Chapnick
Joseph Chelouche
Saul and Jean Chosky
Arta Christiansen

Dale and June Christiansen
Eldad Cidor
William Coblentz
Dov Cognac
Dan, Stacy and Andrew Cohen
Hannah and Norman Cohen
Orna Cohen
Pearl Cohen
Shmulik Cohen
Charles and Paula Collins
Dr. and Mrs. Daniel Collins
Jenny Collins
Catt Condon
Guy Cooper
Anne Copeland
George Craig
Dennis, Barb and Andrew Crossen
Dan Csasznik
Cullen Curtis
Maura Carey Damacion
Yosi De Funes
Sophie Deprez
Shoshana Devora
Marina Devoulin
The Dickman Family
Anthea Disney
Elio and Martha Domeniconi
Kate Doty
Uri Dromi
Oscar Dystel
Lois and Mark Eagleton
Amela Einat
Dr. and Mrs. Richard Eisenberg
Haya Eldar
Huguette Elhadad
Yoav Elkoby
David Engel
The Epstein Family
Tina Essegian

● A cigarette break in Jerusalem's Old City. **RAGHU RAI**

David Fatale
David and Eleanor Fax
The Feldman Family
Maya Feller
Linda Ferrer
Freda and Arnold Finks
Norman and Margot Finks
The Fisher Family
Ronnie Fortis
Michael Fragnito
Adam Frank
Dalia Friedland
Ilan Frieling
David Friend
Peter Friend
Ricki Friesem
Orly Fromer
Barbara Fuscsick
Razi Gaoni
Nelly and Nando Garcon
Anabel Garth
Sharon Geffen
Mattie Genovese
Lou George
Baruch Ghia
Amir Giladi
Allan H. Gill
Yossi Gill
Raanan Gissin
Jocelyne Givon
Sharon Gol
Ronen Golan
Brett Goldberg
The Goldblum Family
Merav Goldenberg
Gil Goldner
Gail Goldstein
Bicky Goldzer
S. Golomb
Micky Gottlieb
Tom Grady
The Grant Family
Steve Gregory
Moshe Gur
Corina Guzman
Klaus Hackel
The Hagerman Family
Yacov Halevi
Benny Halfon
Ardyn and Asnat Halter
Arie Hammer
Moni Haramati
Professor Chaim Harari
Rafi Har-Lev
Hana Hed
Hugh Helm
Eliayahu Hendler
The Higgins Family

Carol Hilder
Paz Himelfarb
Maria Hjelm
Yaffa Hoch
Suzanne Hodgart
Sam Hoffman
Noa Hornik
Stephen Hunt
Orit Inbal
David Innocencio
Mike Isabell
Jeff Jacobsen
Michael Jankelowitz
Giovanna Judge
Margaret Kadoyama
Ita Kafry
Nadav David Kagan
Dr. Madeleine Kahn
Anna Kamdar
Mira Kamdar, Michael and
Alexander Claes
Pete Kamdar
Praveen and Caroline Kamdar
Vinu and Chitra Kamdar
The Kantola Family
Tami Kartin
Dina Kaufman
Tom Keller
Judith Kemp
Tony Kiernan
Dorit Kimche
Nissin Kleinman
Harlan, Sandy and Alexandra Kleiman
Arleen Kline
Hilda Kline
Sammy Knaffo
Nitza Koerner
Tal Korjak
Galia Kornweitz
The Kowaloff Family
Ken Kragen
Jeff Kreindler
Michael Kressbach
The Kuhn Family
Tom Kunhardt
Dr. Joe Kushner
Maxim Kusnetsov
Eliane and Jean Pierre Laffont
Shlomo "Cheech" Lahat
Tsiki Laks
Mr. and Mrs. Stuart Lamb
Stuart M. Lamb, Jr.
Arnon Lande
Ayelet Lavy
Meiri Lavy
Neta Lavy
Tzuf Lavy
Frances Lee

Pat Leizerovitch
Yossi Leshem
Dalia Lev
Michal Levav
The Levick Family
Richard Levick
Maita Levine
Nate Levine
The Levinson Family
Zvi Levran
A. Levy
Meir Levy
Boris Liberman
Laini Liberman
Oded Lifschitz
Heather Lindquist
Dorit Lior
Ziva Livaatan
The Lloyd Family
Barbara Loren
Russ Lowe
Leonard Lueras
Brian Lurie
The Lurie Family
Peter Macchia
Dayna Macy
Ariela Mader
Carol Mann
Akram Mansour
Reda Mansour
Shmuel Mantinband
Yael Maoz
Yaacov Margolin
Brenda Marsh
The McAlpin Family
Holloway McCandless and Family
The McLaughlin Family
Ofer Mechtinger

Doug, Teresa and Paolo Menuez
Robert Messman
Pedro Meyer
Didier Millet
Jonathan Mills
Gila Mintkevich
Ida Mintz
Alberto Mirkin
Toby Momtaz
Scott Montgomery
Lara Morris
Reverend Colin Morton
Ann Moscicki
Alice Moyal
Mohammed Musalem
Freddy Naftali
Matthew and Sascha Naythons
Orit Nevo
Lynne Noone

Patrick O'Hare
Brian O'Reilly
Ingrid Oakes
Yehuda Ofer
Arthur Ollman
Ehud Olmert
Dan Oshima
Julie Osler
John Owen
Allan Pakes
Jack and Gertrude Parker
Gidon Patt
Michael Pazdon
Sara Pearl
Kirsten Stoffregen Pedersen
The Pedersen Family
Rivka Peled
Noam Peleg
Pilar Perez
Gabe and Pat Perle
Kari Perin
Yossi Perlovitch
Gali Perzner-Hacarmeli
Richard L. Peters
The Peters Family
Steve Peterson
The Pledge Family
Ran Plotnizky
Joseph Pokorny
Guy Poran
Deena Porat
Shai Porat
Meir Porush
John Pruzanski
Leah Rabin
Dr. Bob and Paulanne Rabkin
Michael Rand
Eran Rapoport
Zvi Raviv

● A young shepherd in Fassuta. **YEHOSHUA GLOTMAN**

● A Torah scribe in Jerusalem. **NICK KELSH**

FRIENDS AND ADVISORS

● Tel Aviv's beachfront cafe scene. **BARRY SUNDERMEIER**

Menachem Ravivi
Michal Raz
Yaron Raz
Leon Recanati
Abu Rifat Family
The Riklin Family
Anne Rogers
Yitzhak Rogow
Roo
Noah Rosen
Mike and Mindy Rosenberg
Abraham Rosental
Daniel Rossing
Barak Rotem
Natan Rotenberg
Dan Roth and Bonnie Solow
Belle Rubenstein
Scott and Bao Sagan
Tzahal Sagiv
Marianne Samenko
Laurie Samet
Joanna Samuels
Curt Sanburn
James Sano
Noemi Sarel
The Scheldt Family
Zohar Schlesinger
Amos Schocken
Dr. Leonard and Millie Schwartz
Steve Scott
Dave and Rob Scypinski
The Segal Family
Fiona Semberg
Adi Semel
Mirella Sermoneta
Jean Sessa
Yehuda Shafir

Alicia Shahaf
Israel Shalev
Michael Shampanier
Yaacov Shaoulian
Belle Shapiro
Menachem Sharon
Nati Sharoni
Shabtai Shay
Tali Shchori
The Sherman Family
Nancy Shuman
Minnette Siegel
Ted Silverman
David Sinay
Aliza Sivan
Amiram Sivan
Edwin and Dina Slonim

Diana Smith
Ayelet Solomon
The Solovay Family
Jan Sommerville
Jan Starr
Cheryl Stein
Eric Steinberg, Lisa Miller and Family
Aviva Stelberg
Michele Stephenson
Ian Stern
Teri Stewart
Didier Stroz
Eric Sultan
John and Pauline Sundermeier
Sissy Swig
Professor Zeev Tadmore
Yossi Tal-Gan
Alon Talmi
Jon Tandler
The Taylor Family
Sarah Timewell
Drorit Tomer
Frank Trapper
Amir Turetz
Edith Turner
Ella Tvik
Avi Varsano
Motti Verses
Doron Victor
Walter and Eva Vogel
Ziv Volk
Samara Wacks
Colin Wade
Doron Wagner
Keri Walker
Charles Ward
Ed Weiger

Eric, Janet and Lael Weyenberg
Yaron Weinberg
Gilad Weingarten
Michael Welch
Kevin Weldon
Ariel Whetstone
Jerome White
Efraim Yaacobi
Nisan Yanko
Hen Yannay
Nachum Yardeni
Yitzchak Yitzchak
Betsy Young
Yair Youtzis
Trisha Ziff
Ella & Giton Zirich
Chaim Zucker
Shmuel Zurel

ORGANIZATIONS

Academy Travel Ltd.
Apple Center Tel Aviv/Europe House
Archaeological Seminars
Ben Gurion Airport Security
Business Center, Hilton Hotel
BWC Imaging Labs
Camera Obscura School of Art
Delta Film Ltd.
Haskin Press
Hi Fi Lab
Holiday Inn Crowne Plaza, Jerusalem
IDF Spokesman
InnerAsia Expeditions
JDC Israel
Keren Restaurant
Kinko's
Kodak AG Stuttgart
Light Waves
Lufthansa German Airlines
Marina Super
Media Vault
Mivan Overseas Ltd.
Modern Effects
New Lab
Office of the Mayor of Tel Aviv-Jaffa
Pelled Advertising & Promotion Ltd.
Sahar Investments
Shmiel Catering
TWA Airlines

● Men and women at the gates of ultra-religous Mea Shearim in Jerusalem.
NICK KELSH

A Day in the Life of Israel Bibliography

Abu-Fadil, Magda. "Israel's Metals Recoil in 'Boomeranged' Economy." *American Metal Market* (July 19, 1993): 7.

Atkins, Norman. *Jerusalem.* APA Publications (HK) Ltd., 1988.

Atlas, Riva. "Israel Goes Capitalist." *Forbes* (September 13, 1993): 133-134.

Ben-Dov, Meir; Naor, Mordechai and Aner, Zeev. *The Western Wall.* Jerusalem, Israel: Ministry of Defense Publishing House, 1984.

Ben-Zadok, Efraim, ed. *Local Communities and the Israeli Polity.* Albany: State University of New York Press, 1993.

Bernstein, Charles. "American Chains Invade Israel." *Restaurants & Institutions* (February 1, 1994): 18-19.

Bloch, Hana, and Mitchell, Stephen, ed. *The Selected Poetry of Yehuda Amichai.* New York: HarperPerennial, 1992.

"Develop Exports of Cattle Breeding Stock." *Israel Business* (October 1990): 8.

Devir, Ori. *Off the Beaten Track in Israel: A Guide to Beautiful Places.* New York: Adama Books, 1989.

Elon, Amos. *Jerusalem: City of Mirrors.* London: HarperCollins Publishers, 1991.

Encyclopedia Judaica. Jerusalem, Israel: Encyclopedia Judaica Israel/The Macmillan Company Keter Publishing House Ltd., 1972.

Essing, Harry, and Siegle, Abraham. *Israel Today.* New York: Union of American Hebrew Congregations, 1968.

Facts About Israel. Jerusalem, Israel: Ministry of Foreign Affairs, 1979.

"From Russia with Brains." *The Economist* (August 21, 1993): 53.

"Galilean Pink Salmon." *ICEN* (April 12, 1991): 6.

Gibbs, Nancy. "Yitzhak Rabin & Yasser Arafat." *Time* (January 3, 1994): 38-44.

Gleick, Elizabeth. "Requiem for a Hero: The Jews on Oskar Schindler's List Remember Their Unlikely Savior." *People Weekly* (March 21, 1994): 40-45.

Greenwood, Naftali, ed. *Israel Yearbook and Almanac 1994.* Jerusalem: Israel Business, Research, and Technical Translation/Documentation Ltd., 1994.

Grossman, David. *Sleeping on a Wire: Conversations with Palestinians in Israel.* New York: Carol Publishing Group, 1992.

Gutman, Israel (Editor-in-Chief.) *Encyclopedia of the Holocaust.* New York: Macmillan Publishing Company, 1990.

Highlights of the CJF 1990 National Jewish Population Survey. New York: Council of Jewish Federations, 1991.

Himelstein, Rabbi Dr. Shmuel. *The Jewish Primer.* Jerusalem: The Jerusalem Publishing House, Ltd., 1990.

Hoffman, Mark S. *The World Almanac and Book of Facts.* New York: Pharos Books, 1992.

"Industry to Fight 'Pork Law.'" *ICEN* (November 23, 1990): 13.

"Israel: High Technology Leader." *Forbes* (September 13): 127-142.

Keneally, Thomas. *Schindler's List.* New York: Simon and Schuster, 1982.

Kustanowitz, Shuly. "Nazareth Area Readies for Influx of Pilgrims in Year 2000." *Travel Weekly* (December 13, 1993): 64.

Kustanowitz, Shuly, "Tourism Chief: New Water Source Will Boost Desert Development" *Travel Weekly* (April 26, 1993): 71-72.

Landau, David. *Piety and Power: The World of Jewish Fundamentalism.* New York: Hill and Wang, 1993.

Livneh, Micha, and Meshel, Ze'ev. *Masada.* Tel Aviv, Israel: National Parks Authority/Japeth Printing Press Ltd.

Lorch, Netanel. *The Knesset.* Jerusalem: Israel Museum Products Ltd., 1988.

Massdil, Stephen W., Editor. *The Jewish Travel Guide 1993.* London: Jewish Chronicle Publications, 1993.

"McDonald's Breaks Potato Monopoly, with Plans to Build Own Plant in Israel." *Quick Frozen Foods International* (July 1993): 43.

Melman, Yossi. *The New Israelis: An Intimate View of a Changing People.* New York: Farrar, Straus and Giroux, 1993.

Norris, Robert S., and Arkin, William M., "New Base in the Mediterranean?" *Bulletin of the Atomic Scientists* (January-February 1994): 64.

Orni, Efraim, and Efrat, Elisia. *Geography of Israel.* Jerusalem, Israel: Israel Universities Press, 1973.

"Overview of the Israeli Dairy Market." *Agra Europe* (March 31, 1994): 4-5.

Peres, Shimon. *The New Middle East.* New York: Henry Holt and Company, 1993.

"Pig Growers Demand Compensation." *ICEN* (January 18, 1991): 5.

"Pigheaded Protest." *Time* (December 3, 1990): 79.

"Poultry Subsidies to Drop." *ICEN* (April 12, 1991): 6.

Prieto, Victor G., "Israel: From Desert to Flowering Garden." *Agribusiness Worldwide,* (January-February, 1993): 17-21.

Reid, Carlton. *Berlitz Discover Israel.* Oxford: Berlitz Publishing Co., Ltd., 1993.

Scales, Ian. "Israel: Making the Right Connections." *Communications International* (September 1993): 33-34.

"Settlements Fight for Production Quotas." *Israel Business* (March 1990): 5.

"Signed, at Last: Israel and the PLO." *The Economist* (May 7, 1994): 44-46.

Silver, Eric. "A Crook, a Womanizer and a Hero: Israelis Await the Movie 'Schindler's List.'" *Maclean's* (January 17, 1994): 52.

Sudilovsky, Judith, "Golden Crown for Historic Dome of the Rock." *American Metal Market* (April 27, 1994): 7.

Sudilovsky, Judith. "Palestinian, Israeli Steel Trade Blooms." *American Metal Market* (January 4, 1994): 1-2.

Tatcher, Oren, ed. *Let's Go: The Budget Guide to Israel & Egypt 1994.* New York: St. Martin's Press, 1994.

Tilbury, Neil. *Israel: A Travel Survival Kit.* Hawthorne: Lonely Planet Publications., 1992.

Vilnay, Zev. *The Guide to Israel.* Jerusalem, Israel: Hamaker Press, 1972.

Weir, Shelagh. *The Bedouin.* London: British Museum Publications Ltd., 1990.

Werblowsky, R.J. Zwi, and Wigoder, Geoffrey. *The Encyclopedia of the Jewish Religion.* New York: Holt, Rinehart and Winston, Inc., 1965

"Wild over Wine." *ICEN* (October 11, 1991): 33.

Winter, Dick. *Culture Shock! Israel.* Portland: Graphic Arts Center Publishing Company, 1992.

Women in Israel. Jerusalem: Israel Information Center, 1991.

Yadin, Yigal. *Masada.* London: Weidenfeld and Nicolson, 1967.

Zimmermann, Tim. "A Shaky Start to a Different Picture." *U.S. News & World Report* (May 16, 1994): 14.

SHALOM
SALAAM
PEACE

Top Israeli rock star Shalom Hanoch between takes on a new album he is

Gilgal
Beth Dagon
Lod
Bethel
Ai
Ekron
Jabneel
Ashdod
Ascalon
Gath
Eglon
Lachish
Libnah
Gaza
Tekoa
Halhul
KIRJATH ARBA
(Hebron)
Socoh
Gerar
Beersheba
Besor
Aroer
SIMEON
Beth Marcaboth
Zephath